£1.50

SHOVELLING TROUBLE

Shovelling Trouble is a new collection of essays from the pen of Canada's most stunningly talented wordsmith. Fresh from the success of his latest novel *St. Urbain's Horseman,* Mordecai Richler here casts his penetratingly perceptive eye over the pearls and the swine, the flotsam and jetsam of our time.

With subject matter ranging from Timothy Leary and James Bond to modern Germany and life in the cafe society of post-war Paris, Richler covers the field and plays no favourites; always true to his convictions, often devastatingly witty, but never trivial.

Mordecai Richler was born in Montreal in 1931. His first novel, *The Acrobats* was published in 1954, and since then he has become one of Canada's most widely known and critically acclaimed authors, receiving in the course of his literary career two Governor-General of Canada's Awards. His best-selling books include *St. Urbain's Horseman, Cocksure, The Street,* and *Hunting Tigers Under Glass.*

ALSO BY MORDECAI RICHLER

The Acrobats
Son of a Smaller Hero
A Choice of Enemies
The Apprenticeship of Duddy Kravitz
The Incomparable Atuk
Cocksure
Hunting Tigers Under Glass
The Street
St. Urbain's Horseman
Canadian Writing Today (editor)

SHOVELLING TROUBLE

MORDECAI RICHLER

QUARTET BOOKS LONDON

First published in Great Britain by Quartet Books Limited 1973
27 Goodge Street, London W.1

Copyright © 1972 McClelland and Stewart Limited

ISBN 0 704 32001 0

Made and printed in Great Britain by Cox and Wyman Limited, London, Fakenham and Reading.

Why I Write 1

A Sense of the Ridiculous 13

Gordon Craig 39

Bond 49

The Holocaust and After 81

Making It 95

Huckleberry Finklestone 101

Starting Out in the Thirties 105

Porky's Plaint 111

Answering the Ads 117

Games (Some) People Play 133

Not Me, Leary, Not Me 137

Following the Babylonian Talmud, After Maimonides . . . Rabbi Stuart Rosenberg on the History of the Jewish Community in Canada 143

Maple Leaf Culture Time 149

'Etes-vous canadien?' 155

Acknowledgements 161

For Jon and Carmen

SHOVELLING TROUBLE

WHY I WRITE

As I write, October 1970, I have just finished a novel of intimidating length, a fiction begun five years ago, on the other side of the moon, so I am, understandably enough, concerned by the state of the novel in general. Is it dead? Dead *again*. Like God or MGM. Father McLuhan says so (writing, "The Age of Writing has passed") and Dylan Thomas's daughter recently pronounced stingingly from Rome, 'Nobody reads novels any more.'

I'm soon going to be forty. Too old to learn how to teach. Or play the guitar. Stuck, like the blacksmith, with the only craft I know. But brooding about the novel, and its present unmodishness, it's not the established practitioner I'm grieving for, it's the novice, that otherwise effervescent young man stricken with the wasting disease whose earliest symptom is the first novel. These are far from halcyon days for the fledgling novelist.

Look at it this way. Most publishers, confronted with a rectal polyp, hold on to hope, tempting the surgeon with a bigger advance. They know the score. What's truly terminal. Offered a first novel or worse news – *infamy* – a short story collection, they call for the ledgers which commemorate last

1

season's calamities. The bright new talents nobody wanted to read. Now more to be remaindered than remembered, as *Time* once observed.

I know. Carting off my cumbersome manuscript to be xeroxed, it was my first novel that was uppermost in my mind, *The Acrobats,* published in 1954, when I was twenty-three years old. At the time, I was living in Montreal, and my British publisher, André Deutsch, urged me to visit his Canadian distributor before sailing for England. So I caught the overnight Greyhound bus to Toronto, arriving at 7 a.m. in a city where I knew nobody and walking the sweltering summer streets until 9.30, when offices would open.

The Canadian distributor, bracingly realistic, did not detain me overlong with *recherché* chitchat about style, content or influences. 'Have you written a thick book or a thin book?' he demanded.

A thin one, I allowed.

'Thick books sell better than thin ones here.'

A slow learner, I published five more before I at last surfaced with a thick one, *St. Urbain's Horseman,* which was all of 180,000 words. And retrieving my seven xeroxed copies, I couldn't help but reflect that the £80 I forked out for them was only slightly less than the British advance against royalties I was paid for my first novel sixteen years ago. The American publisher, G. P. Putnam's Sons, was more generous; they sent me 750 dollars. But I was disheartened when I received their catalogue. Putnam's was, at the time, trying a new experiment in book selling. If you didn't enjoy one of their books, your bookseller would return you the money, no questions asked. Only two books listed in the autumn catalogue conspicuously failed to carry this guarantee, mine, and another young writer's.

The Acrobats ultimately sold some 2,000 copies in England and less than 1,000 in the U.S., but it was – as I pointed out to my aunt, on a visit to Montreal – translated into five foreign languages.

'There must,' she said, smoothing out her skirt, 'be a shortage of books.'

My uncle, also a critic, was astonished when he computed my earnings against the time I had invested. I would have earned more mowing his lawn, and, furthermore, it would have been healthier for me.

The novel, the novel.

Write a study of the Pre-Columbian butterfly, compose an account of colonial administration in Tonga, and Nigel Dennis, that most perspicacious and witty of British reviewers, might perversely enshrine it in a 1,000 word essay in the *Sunday Telegraph*. Or Malcolm Muggeridge might take it as the text for a lengthy sermon, excoriating once more that generation of younger vipers who will continue to enjoy, enjoy, after he has passed on to his much-advertised rest. But novels, coming in batches of twenty weekly, seldom rate a notice of their own in England. Sixteen are instant losers. Or, looked at another way, payola from the literary editor. Badly-paid reviewer's perks. The reviewer is not even expected to read them, but it is understood he can flog them for half-price to a buyer from Fleet Street. Of the four that remain, comprising the typical novel column, one is made especially for skewering in the last deadly paragraph, and two are destined for the scales of critical balance. On the one hand, somewhat promising, on the other, ho-hum. Only one makes the lead. But it must lead in four of the five influential newspapers, say, the *Sunday Times, Observer, The Times* and *Guardian,* if anybody's to take notice. Some even buying.

'Basically,' a concerned New York editor told me, 'the trouble is we are trying to market something nobody wants. Or needs.'

The novel has had its day, we are assured, and in the Age of Aquarius, film, man, film's the stuff that will do more than fiction can to justify God's way to man. Given any rainy afternoon who wants to read Doris Lessing fully-clothed for forty bob when, for only ten, you can actually see Jane Fonda starkers, shaking it for you and art, and leaving you with sufficient change for a half-bottle of gin?

To be fair, everything has (and continues) to be tried. Novels like decks of playing cards. Shuffle, and read it anyway it comes up. Novels like jokes or mutual funds. You cut your potential time-investment loss by inviting everybody in the office to pound out a chapter. *Naked Came The Stranger. I Knew Daisy Smutten.* Or instead-of-sex. Why weary yourself, performing badly perhaps when, if only you lose yourself in *The Adventurers*, you can have better-hung Dax come for you? And, sooner or later, somebody's bound to turn to the cassette. No need to bruise your thumbs turning pages. You slip the thing into a machine and listen to Raquel Welch read it. 'The latest Amis as read by . . .'

On a recent visit to Canadian university campuses, I found myself a creature to be pitied, still writing novels when anybody could tell you that's no longer 'where it's at'. But I've tried the logical alternative, screen writing, and though I still write for the films from time to time, it's not really for me.

The trouble is, like most novelists, I am conditioned to working for years on material I discuss with nobody. To adjust from that to script writing is too much like what Truman Capote once described as group sports. Even so, five years in a room with a novel-in-progress can be more than gruelling. If getting up to it some mornings is a pleasure, it is, just as often, a punishment. A self-inflicted punishment. There have been false starts, wrong turns, and weeks with nothing to show except sharpened pencils and bookshelves re-arranged. I have rewritten chapters ten times that in the end simply didn't belong and had to be cut. Ironically, even unforgivably, it usually seems to be those passages over which I have laboured most arduously, nurtured in the hothouse, as it were, that never really spring to life, and the pages that came too quickly, with utterly suspect ease, that read most felicitously.

Riding into my second year on *St. Urbain's Horseman*, disheartened by proliferating school bills, diminished savings, and only fitful progress, I finally got stuck so badly that there was nothing for it but to shove the manuscript aside. I started in on another novel, a year's heat, which yielded *Cocksure*. Anthony Burgess clapped hands in *Life, Time* approved, *Newsweek* cheered, and the British notices were almost uniformly fulsome. Encouraged and somewhat solvent again, I resolved to resume work on *Horseman*. After twelve years in London, I was to return to Montreal for a year with my wife and five children, to report for duty as writer-in-residence at Sir George Williams University, my *alma mater*. Or, put plainly, in return for taking a 'creative writing' seminar one afternoon a week, I could get on with my novel, comparatively free of financial worry.

Ostensibly, conditions were ideal, winds couldn't be more favourable, and so I started in for the ninth time on page one of *St. Urbain's Horseman*. I didn't get much further before, my stomach crawling with fear, I began to feel I'd lost something somewhere.

I got stuck. Morning after morning, I'd switch to an article or a book review, already long overdue. Or compose self-pitying letters to friends. Or dawdle until eleven a.m., when it was too late to make a decent start on anything, and I was at last free to quit my room and stroll downtown. St. Catherine Street. Montreal's Main Stem, as the doyen of our gossip columnists has it. Pretending to browse for books by lesser novelists, I could surreptitiously check out the shops on stacks of the paperback edition of *Cocksure*.

Or take in a movie maybe.

Ego dividends. I could pick a movie that I had been asked to write myself, but declined. Whatever the movie, it was quite likely I would know the director or the script writer, maybe even one of the stars.

So there you have it. Cat's out of the bag. In London, I skitter on the periphery of festooned circles, know plenty of inside stories. Bomb-shells. Like which cabinet minister is an insatiable pederast. What best-selling novel was really stitched together by a cunning editor. Which wrinkled Hollywood glamour queen is predisposed towards gang shags with hirsute Neapolitan waiters from the Mirabelle. Yes, yes, I'll own up to it. I am, after eighteen years as a writer, not utterly unconnected or unknown, as witness the entry in the indispensable *Oxford Companion to Canadian Literature*.

> Richler, Mordecai (1931—) Born in Montreal, he was educated at Sir George Williams College and spent two years abroad. Returning to Canada in 1952, he joined the staff of the Canadian Broadcasting Corporation. He now lives in England, where he writes film scripts, novels, and short stories. The key to Richler's novels is . . .

After eighteen years and six novels there is nothing I cherish so much as the first and most vulnerable book, *The Acrobats*, not only because it marked the first time my name appeared in a Canadian newspaper, a prescient Toronto columnist writing from London, 'You've not heard of Mordecai Richler yet, but, look out, she's a name to watch for'; but also because it was the one book I could write as a totally private act, with the deep, inner assurance that nobody would be such a damn fool as to publish it. That any editor would boot it back to me, a condescending rejection note enclosed, enabling me to quit Paris for Montreal, an honourable failure, and get down to the serious business of looking for a job. A real job.

I did in fact return to Montreal, broke, while my manuscript made the rounds. My father, who hadn't seen me for two years, took me out for a drive.

'I hear you wrote a novel in Europe,' he said.

'Yes.'

'What's it called?'

'*The Acrobats*.'

'What in the hell do you know about the circus?'

I explained the title was a symbolic one.

'Is it about Jews or ordinary people?' my father asked.

To my astonishment, André Deutsch offered to publish the novel. Now, when somebody asked me what I did, I could reply, without seeming fraudulent to myself, that I was indeed a writer. If, returned to Hampstead once more, I still tended to doubt it in the early morning hours, now *The Acrobats*, in shop windows here and there, was the proof I needed. My novel on display side by side with real ones. There is no publication as agonizing or charged with elation as the first.

Gradually, you assume that what you write will be published. After the first book, composing a novel is no longer self-indulgent, a conceit. It becomes, among other things, a living. Though to this day reviews can still sting or delight, it's sales that buy you the time to get on with the next. Mind you, there are a number of critics whose esteem I prize, whose opprobrium can sear, but, for the most part, I, in common with other writers, have learned to read reviews like a market report. This one will help move the novel, that one not.

Writing a novel, as George Orwell has observed, is a horrible, exhausting struggle. 'One would never undertake such a thing if one were not driven by some demon whom one can neither resist nor understand.' Something else. Each novel is a failure, or there would be no compulsion to begin afresh. Critics don't help. Speaking as someone who fills that office on occasion, I must say that the critic's essential relationship is with the reader, not the writer. It is his duty to celebrate good books, eviscerate bad ones, lying ones.

When I first published, in 1954, it was commonly assumed that to commit a film script was to sell out (Daniel Fuchs, Christopher Isherwood, Irwin Shaw), and that the good and dedicated life was in academe. Now, the inverse seems to be the Canadian and, I daresay, American case. The creative young yearn to be in films, journeymen retire to the universities: *seems* to be the case, because, happily, there are exceptions.

All of us tend to romanticize the world we nearly chose. In my case, academe, where instead of having to bring home the meat, I would only be obliged to stamp it, rejecting this shoulder of beef as Hank James derivative, or that side of pork as sub-Jimmy Joyce. I saw myself no longer a perplexed free-lancer with an unpredictable income, balancing this magazine assignment, that film job, against the time it would buy me. No sir. Sipping Tio Pepe in the faculty club, snug in my leather winged-back armchair and the company of other disinterested scholars, I would not, given the assurance of a monthly cheque, chat about anything so coarse as money.

– Why don't you, um, write a novel yourself this summer, Professor Richler?

– Well, Dr. Lemming, like you, I have too much respect for the tradition to sully it with my own feeble scribblings.

– Quite.

– Just so.

Alas, academe, like girls, whisky, and literature, promised better than it paid. I now realize, after having ridden the academic gravy train for a season, that vaudeville hasn't disappeared or been killed by TV, but merely retired to small circuits, among them, the universities. Take the Canadian poets, for instance. Applying for Canada Council grants today, they no longer catalogue their publications (the obsolete accomplishments of linear man) but, instead, like TV actors on the make, they list their personal appearances, the campuses where they read aloud. Wowsy at Simon Fraser U., hotsy at Carleton. Working wrinkles out of the act in the stix, with a headliner coming up in the veritable Palace of the Canadian campus circuit, the University of Toronto.

If stand-up comics now employ batteries of gag writers because national TV exposure means they can only use their material once, then professors, playing to a new house every season, can peddle the same oneliners year after year, improving only on timing and delivery. For promos, they publish. Bringing out journals necessary to no known audience, but essential to their advancement.

Put plainly, these days everybody's in show business, all trades are riddled with impurities. And so, after a most enjoyable (and salaried) year in academe – a reverse sabbatical, if you like – I returned to the uncertain world of the free-lance writer, where nobody, as James Thurber once wrote, sits at anybody's feet unless he's been knocked there. I returned with my family to London, no deeper into *St. Urbain's Horseman* than when I left.

Why do you write?

Doctors are seldom asked why they practise, shoemakers how come they cobble, or baseball players why they don't drive a coal truck instead, but again and again writers, like housebreakers, are asked why they do it.

Orwell, as might be expected, supplies the most honest answer in his essay, 'Why I Write.'

'1. Sheer egoism. Desire to seem clever, to be talked about, to be remembered after death, to get your own back on grown-ups who snubbed you in childhood, etc. etc.' To this I would add egoism informed by imagination, style, and a desire to be known, yes, *but only on your own conditions*.

Nobody is more embittered than the neglected writer and, obviously, allowed a certain recognition, I am a happier and more generous man than I would otherwise be. But nothing I have done to win this recognition appals me, has gone against my nature. I fervently believe that all a writer should send into the marketplace to be judged is his own work; the rest should remain private. I deplore the writer as a personality, however large and undoubted the talent, as is the case with Norman Mailer. I also do not believe in special licence for so-called artistic temperament. After all, my problems, as I grudgingly come within spitting distance of middle age, are the same as anybody else's. Easier maybe. I can bend my anxieties to subversive uses. Making stories of them. When I'm not writing, I'm a husband and a father of five. Worried about pollution. The population explosion. My son's report cards.

'2. Aesthetic enthusiasm. Perception of beauty in the external world, or, on the other hand, in words and their right arrangement.' The agonies involved in creating a novel, the unsatisfying draft, the scenes you never get right, are redeemed by those rare and memorable days when, seemingly without reason, everything falls right. Bonus days. Blessed days when, drawing on resources unsuspected, you pluck ideas and prose out of your skull that you never dreamt yourself capable of.

Such, such are the real joys.

Unfortunately, I don't feel that I've ever been able to sustain such flights for a novel's length. So the passages that flow are balanced with those which were forced in the hothouse. Of all the novels I've written, it is *The Apprenticeship of Duddy Kravitz* and *Cocksure* which come closest to my intentions and, therefore, give me the most pleasure. I should add that I'm still lumbered with the characters and ideas, the social concerns I first attempted in *The Acrobats*. Every serious writer has, I think, one theme, many variations to play on it.

Like any serious writer, I want to write one novel that will last, something that will make me remembered after death, and so I'm compelled to keep trying.

'3. Historical impulse. Desire to see things as they are. . . .'

No matter how long I continue to live abroad, I do feel forever rooted in Montreal's St. Urbain Street. That was my time, my place, and I have elected myself to get it right.

'4. Political purpose – using the world "political" in the widest possible sense. Desire to push the world in a certain direction, to alter other people's idea of the kind of society that they should strive after.'

Not an overlarge consideration in my work, though I would say that any serious writer is a moralist and only incidently an entertainer.

After a year on the academic payroll, I returned to London in August 1969, abysmally depressed, because after four years *St. Urbain's Horseman* was no nearer to completion and, once more, my savings were running down. I retired to my room each morning, ostensibly to work, but actually to prepare highly impressive schedules. Starting next Monday, without fail, I would write three pages a day. Meanwhile, I would train for this ordeal by taking a nap every afternoon, followed by trips to the movies I simply had to see, thereby steeling myself against future fatigue and distractions. Next Monday, however, nothing came. Instead, taking the sports pages of the *International Herald-Tribune* as my text, I calculated, based on present standings and won-lost ratios, where each team in both major baseball leagues would end the season. Monday, falling on the eighth of the month, was a bad date, anyway. Neither here nor there. I would seriously begin work, I decided, on the 15th of the month, writing *six* pages daily. After all, if Simenon could write a novel in a week, surely... When I failed to write even a paragraph on the 15th, I was not upset. Finally, I grasped the real nature of my problem. Wrong typewriter. Wrong colour ribbon. Wrong texture paper. I traded in my machine for one with a new type face, bought six blue ribbons, and three boxes of heavy bond paper, but still nothing came. Absolutely nothing.

Then, suddenly, in September, I began to put in long hours in my room, writing with ease, one day's work more gratifying than the next, and within a year the novel was done, all 550 typewritten pages.

The first person to read the manuscript, my wife, was, like all writers' wives, in an invidious position. I depend on my wife's taste and honesty. It is she, unenviably, who must tell me if I've gone wrong. If she disapproved, however diplomatically, there would be angry words, some things I would have to say about her own deficiencies, say her choice of clothes, her cooking, and the mess she was making of raising our children. I would also point out that it was gratuitously cruel of her to laugh aloud in bed, reading *Portnoy's Complaint*, when I was having such a struggle with my own novel. All the same, I would not submit the manuscript. If she found it wanting, I would put it aside for six months to be considered afresh. Another year, another draft. And yet – and yet – even if she proclaimed the manuscript a masterpiece, radiating delight, I would immediately discount her praise, thinking she's only my wife, loyal and loving, and therefore dangerously prejudiced. Maybe a liar. Certainly beyond the critical pale.

After my wife had pronounced, foolishly saying *St. Urbain's Horseman* was the best novel I'd written by far (making me resentful, because this obviously meant she hadn't enjoyed my earlier work as much as she should have done) I submitted the manuscript to my editors. Another hurdle, another intricate relationship. I deal with editors who are commonly taken to be among the most prescient in publishing – Robert Gottlieb at Knopf and, in England, Tony Godwin at Weidenfeld & Nicolson – but once I had sent them my manuscript, and they had obviously not dropped everything to read it overnight, wakening me with fulsome cables, long distance calls, champagne and caviar, I began to arm myself with fancied resentments and the case that could be made against their much-advertised (but as I had reason to suspect) over-rated acumen. As each morning's mail failed to yield a letter, and the telephone didn't ring, I lay seething on the living-room sofa, ticking off, in my mind's eye, all the lesser novelists on their lists, those they flattered with larger ads, bigger first prints, more generous advances, more expensive lunches, than they had ever allowed me. In fact I had all but decided it was time to move on to other, more appreciative publishers when, only a week after I had submitted the manuscript, both editors wrote me enthusiastic letters. Enthusiastic letters, that is, until you have scrutinized them for the ninth time, reading between the lines, and grasp that the compliments are forced, the praise false, and that the sour truth hidden beneath the clichés is that they don't really like the novel. Or even if they did, their taste is demonstrably fallible, and corrupted by the fact that they are personal friends, especially fond of my wife.

Put plainly, nothing helps.

A SENSE OF THE RIDICULOUS
Notes on Paris 1951 and After
For Mason Hoffenberg and Joe Dughi

In the summer of 1967, our very golden EXPO summer, I was drinking with an old and cherished friend at Montreal airport, waiting for my flight to London, when all at once he said, 'You know, I'm going to be forty soon.'

At the time, I was still a smug thirty-six.

'Hell,' he added, whacking his glass against the table, outraged, 'it's utterly ridiculous. Me, forty? My father's forty!'

Though we were both Montrealers, we had first met in Paris in 1951, and we warmed over those days now, *our* movable feast, until my flight was called.

A few days later, back in London, where I had been rooted for more than ten years, I sat sipping coffee on the King's Road, Chelsea, brooding about Paris and watching the girls pass in their minis and high suede boots. Suddenly, hatefully, it struck me that there was a generation younger than mine. Another bunch. And so we were no longer licensed to idle at cafés, to be merely promising as we were in Paris, but were regularly expected to deliver the goods, books and movies to be judged by others. At my age, appointments must be kept, I thought, searching for a taxi.

Time counts.

As it happened, my appointment was with a Star at the Dorchester. The Star, internationally-known, obscenely overpaid, was attended in his suite by a bitch-mother private secretary, a soothing queer architect to keep everybody's glasses filled with chilled Chevalier Montrachet, and, kneeling by the hassock on which big bare feet rested, a chiropodist. The chiropodist, black leather tool box open before him, scissor-filled drawers protruding, black bowler lying alongside on the rug, was kneading the Star's feet, pausing to reverently snip a nail or caress a big toe, lingering whenever he provoked an involuntary little yelp of pleasure.

'I am ever so worried,' the chiropodist said, 'about your returning to Hollywood, Sir.'

'Mmmnnn.' This delivered with eyes squeezed ecstatically shut.

'Who will look after your feet there?'

The Star had summoned me because he wanted to do a picture about the assassination of Leon Trotsky. Trotsky, my hero. 'The way I see it,' he said, 'Trotsky was one of the last really, really great men. Like Louis B. Mayer.'

I didn't take on the screenplay. Instead, on bloody-minded impulse, I bought air tickets and announced to my wife, 'We're flying to Paris tomorrow.'

Back to Paris to be cleansed.

As my original left bank days had been decidedly impecunious, this was something like an act of vengeance. We stayed on the right bank, eating breakfast in bed at the Georges V, dropping into the Dior boutique, doing the galleries, stopping for a fin de maison here and a Perrier there, window-shopping on the rue du Rivoli, dining at Lapérouse, le Tour d'Argent, and le Méditerranée.

Fifteen years had not only made for changes in me.

The seedy Café Royale, on Boul. St. Germain, the terrace once spilling over with rambunctious friends until two in the morning, when the action drifted on to the Mabillion and from there to the notorious Pergola, had been displaced by the sickeningly mod, affluent le Drugstore. In Montparnasse, the Dôme was out of favour again, everybody now gathering at the barn-like La Coupole. Strolling past the Café le Tournot, I no longer recognized the abundantly confident *Paris Review* bunch (the loping Plimpton in his snapbrim fedora, Eugene Walter, Peter Mathiessen) either conferring on the pavement or sprawled on the terrace, dunking croissants into the morning café au lait, always and enviably surrounded by the most appetizing college girls in town. Neither was the affable Richard Wright to be seen any more, working on the pinball machine.

Others, alas, were still drifting from café to café, cruelly winded now, grubbiness no longer redeemed by youth, bald, twitchy, defensive, and embittered. To a man, they had all the faults of genius. They were alienated, of course, as well as being bad credit risks, rent-skippers, prodigious drinkers or junkies, and reprobates, and yet – and yet – they had been left behind, unlucky or not sufficiently talented. They made me exceedingly nervous, for now they appeared embarrassing, like fat bachelors of fifty tooling about in fire-engine red MGs or women in their forties flouncing their mini-skirts.

The shrill, hysterical editor of one of the little magazines of the Fifties caught up with me. 'I want you to know,' he said, 'that I rejected all that crap Terry Southern is publishing in America now.'

Gently, I let on that Terry and I were old friends.

'Jimmy Baldwin,' he said, 'has copied all my gestures. If you see him on TV, it's me,' he shrieked. 'It's me.'

On balance, our weekend in Paris was more unsettling than satisfying. Seated at the Dôme, well-dressed, consuming double scotches rather than nursing a solitary beer on the lookout for somebody who had just cashed his GI cheque on the black market, I realized I appeared just the sort of tourist who would have aroused the unfeeling scorn of the boy I had been in 1951. A scruffy boy with easy, bigoted attitudes, encouraging a beard, addicted to T-shirts, the obligatory blue jeans and, naturally, sandals. Absorbed by the Tarot and trying to write in the manner of Céline. Given to wild pronouncements about Coca-Cola culture and late nights listening to Sydney Bechet at the Vieux Colombier. We had not yet been labelled beats, certainly not hippies. Rather, we were taken for existentialists by *Life*, if not by Jean-Paul Sartre, who had a sign posted in a jazz cellar warning he had nothing whatsoever to do with these children and that they hardly represented his ideas.

I frequently feel I've lost something somewhere. Spontaneity maybe, or honest appetite. In Paris all I ever craved for was to be accepted as a serious novelist one day, seemingly an impossible dream. Now I'm harnessed to this ritual of being a writer, shaking out the morning mail for cheque-size envelopes – scanning the newspapers – breakfast – then upstairs to work. To try to work.

If I get stuck, if it turns out an especially sour, unyielding morning, I will recite a lecture to myself that begins, Your father had to be out at six every morning, driving to the junk yard in the sub-zero dark, through Montreal blizzards. You work at home, never at your desk before nine, earning more for a day's remembered insults than your father ever made, hustling scrap, in a week.

Or I return, in my mind's eye, to Paris.

Paris, the dividing line. Before Paris, experience could be savoured for its own immediate satisfactions. It was total. Afterwards, I became cunning, a writer, somebody with a use for everything, even intimacies.

I was only a callow kid of nineteen when I arrived in Paris in 1951, and so it was, in the truest sense, my university. St. Germain des Prés was my campus, Montparnasse my frat house, and my two years there are a sweetness I retain, as others do wistful memories of McGill or Oxford. Even now,

I tend to measure my present conduct against the rules I made for myself in Paris.

The first declaration to make about Paris is that we young Americans, and this Canadian, didn't go there so much to discover Europe as to find and reassure each other, who were separated by such vast distances at home. Among the as yet unknown young writers in Paris at the time, either friends or nodding café acquaintances, there were Terry Southern, Alan Temko, Alfred Chester, Herbert Gold, David Burnett, Mavis Gallant, Alexander Trocchi, Christopher Logue, Mason Hoffenberg, James Baldwin, and the late David Stacton.

About reputations.

A few years ago, after I had spoken at one of those vast synagogue-cum-community plants that have supplanted the pokey little *shuls* of my Montreal boyhood, all-pervasive deodorant displacing the smell of pickled herring, a lady shot indignantly out of her seat to say, 'I'm sure you don't remember me, but we were at school together. Even then you had filthy opinions, but who took you seriously? Nobody. *Can you please tell me,*' she demanded, '*why on earth anybody takes you seriously now?*'

Why, indeed? If only she knew how profoundly I agreed with her. For I, too, am totally unable to make that imaginative leap that would enable me to accept that anybody I grew up with – or, in this case, cracked peanuts with at the Mabillion – or puffed pot with at the Old Navy – could now be mistaken for a writer. A reputation.

In 1965, when Alexander Trocchi enjoyed a season in England as a sort of Dr. Spock of pot, pontificating about how good it was for you on one in-depth TV discussion after another, I was hard put to suppress an incredulous giggle each time his intelligent, craggy face filled the screen. I am equally unconvinced, stunned even, when I see Terry Southern's or Herb Gold's picture in *Time*.

I also find it disheartening that, in the end, writers are no less status-conscious than the middle-class they – we, I should say – excoriate with such appetite. As my high school friends, the old Sunday morning scrub team, has been split by economics, this taxi driver's boy now a fat suburban cat, that tailor's son still ducking bailiffs in a one-man basement factory, so we, who pretended to transcend such matters, have, over the demanding years, been divided by reputations. If our yardstick is more exacting, it still measures without mercy, coarsening the happy time we once shared.

Paris.

It would be nice, it would be tidy, to say with hindsight that we were a group, knit by political anger or a literary policy or even an aesthetic revulsion for all things American, but the truth was we recognized each other by no more than a shared sense of the ridiculous. And so we passed many a languorous, pot-filled afternoon on the terrace of the Dôme or the Selecte, improvising, not unlike jazz groups, on the hot news from America, where Truman was yielding to Eisenhower. We bounced an inanity to and fro, until, magnified through bizarre extension, we had disposed of it as an absurdity. We invented obscene quiz shows for television, and ad-libbed sexual outrages that could be interpolated into a John Marquand novel, a Norman Rockwell *Post* cover, or a June Allyson movie. The most original innovator and wit amongst us was easily the deceptively, gentle Mason Hoffenberg, and one way or another we all remain indebted to him.

Oddly, I cannot recall that we ever discussed 'our stuff' with each other. In fact, a stranger noting our cultivated indifference, the cool café posture, could never have guessed that when we weren't shuffling from café to café, in search of girls – a party – any diversion – we were actually labouring hard and long at typewriters in cramped, squalid hotel rooms, sending off stories to America, stories that rebounded with a sickening whack. The indifference to success was feigned, our café cool was false, for the truth is we were real Americans, hungering for recognition and its rewards, terrified of failure.

The rules of behaviour, unwritten, were nevertheless rigid.

It was not considered corrupt to take a thousand dollars from Girodias to write a pornographic novel under a pseudonym for the tourist trade, but anybody who went home to commit a thesis was automatically out. We weighed one another not by our backgrounds or prospects, but by taste, the books we kept by our bedside. Above all, we cherished the unrehearsed response, the zany personality, and so we prized many a bohemian dolt or exhibitionist, the girl who dyed her hair orange or kept a monkey for a pet, the most defiant queen, or the sub-Kerouac who wouldn't read anything because it might influence his style. Looked at another way, you were sure to know somebody who would happily bring on an abortion with a hat pin or turn you on heroin or peddle your passport, but nobody at all you could count on to behave decently if you were stuck with your Uncle Irv and Aunt Sophie, who were 'doing Europe' this summer.

Each group its own conventions, which is to say we were not so much non-conformists as subject to our own peculiar conformities or, if you like, anti-bourgeois inversions. And so, if you were going to read a fat Irwin Shaw, a lousy best-seller, you were safest concealing it under a Marquis de Sade jacket. What I personally found most trying was the necessity to choke enthusiasm, never to reveal elation, when the truth was I was out of my mind with joy to be living in Paris, actually living in Paris, France.

My room at the Grand Hotel Excelsior, off the Boul' Mich, was filled with rats, rats and a gratifying depraved past, for the hotel had once functioned as a brothel for the Wehrmacht. Before entering my room, I hollered, and whacked on the door, hoping to scatter the repulsive little beasts. Before putting on my sweater, I shook it out for rat droppings. But lying on my lumpy bed, ghetto-liberated, a real expatriate, I could read the forbidden, outspoken Henry Miller, skipping the windy cosmic passages, warming to the hot stuff. Paris in the fabled twenties, when luscious slavering American school teachers came over to seek out artists like me, begging for it.

Waylaying randy old Henry in public toilets, seizing him by the cock. Scratching on his hotel room door, entering to gobble him. *Wherever I travel I'm too late. The orgy has moved elsewhere.*

My father wrote, grabbing for me across the seas to remind me of my heritage. He enclosed a Jewish calendar, warning me that Rosh Hashonnah came early this year, even for me who smoked hashish on the sabbath. Scared even as I smoked it, but more terrified of being put down as chicken-shit. My father wrote to say that the YMHA *Beacon* was sponsoring a short story contest and that the *Reader's Digest* was in the market for 'Unforgettable Characters'. Meanwhile, the *New Yorker* wouldn't have me, neither would the *Partisan Review*.

Moving among us, there was the slippery, eccentric Mr. Soon. He was, he said, the first Citizen of the World. He had anticipated Gary Davis, who was much in the news then. Mussolini had deported Mr. Soon from Italy, even as he had one of our underground heroes, the necromancer Aleister Crowley, The Great Beast 666, but the Swiss had promptly shipped Mr. Soon back again. He had no papers. He had a filthy, knotted beard, a body seemingly fabricated of Meccano parts, the old clothes and cigarettes we gave him, and a passion for balaclavas. The police were always nabbing him for questioning. They wanted to know about drug addiction and foreigners who had been in Paris for more than three months without a *carte d'identité*. Mr. Soon became an informer.

'And what,' he'd ask, 'do you think of the poetry of Mao Tse-tung?'

'Zingy.'

'And how,' he'd ask, 'does one spell your name?'

My American friends were more agitated than I, a non-draftable Canadian, about the Korean War. We sat on the terrace of the Mabillion, drunkenly accumulating beer coasters, on the day General Ridgeway drove into Paris, replacing Eisenhower at SHAPE. Only a thin bored crowd of the curious turned out to look over the general from Korea, yet the gendarmes were everywhere, and the boulevard was black with Gardes Mobiles, their fierce polished helmets catching the sun. All at once, the Place de l'Odeon was clotted with communist demonstrators, men, women and boys, squirting out of the backstreets, whipping out broomsticks from inside their shapeless jackets and hoisting anti-American posters on them.

'RIDGEWAY,' the men hollered.

'*A la porte,*' the women responded in a piercing squeal.

Instantly the gendarmes penetrated the demonstration, fanning out, swinging the capes that were weighed down with lead, cracking heads, and smashing noses. The once disciplined cry of *Ridgeway, à la porte!*, faltered, then broke. Demonstrators retreated, scattering, clutching their bleeding faces.

A German general, summoned by NATO, came to Paris, and French Jews and socialists paraded in sombre silence down the Champs Elysées, wearing striped pyjamas, their former concentration camp uniforms. A Parisian Jewish couple I had befriended informed me at dinner that their new-born boy would not be circumcised, 'Just in case.' The Algerian troubles had begun. There was a war on in what we then called Indo-China. The gendarmes began to raid left bank hotels one by one, looking for Arabs without papers. Six o'clock in the morning they would pound on your door, open it, and demand to see your passport. 'I am a c-c-c-itizen of the world,' said Greenblatt, at that time something called a non-figurative poet, now with Desilu Productions.

One night the virulently anti-communist group, Paix et Liberté, pasted up posters everywhere that showed a flag, the Hammer and Sickle, flying from the top of the Eiffel Tower. HOW WOULD YOU LIKE TO SEE THIS? the caption read. Early the next morning the communists went from poster to poster and pasted the Stars and Stripes over the Russian flag.

With Joe Dughi, a survivor of Normandy and the Battle of the Bulge, who was taking the course on French Civilization at the Sorbonne, I made the long trip to a flaking working-class suburb to see the Russian propaganda feature film, *Meeting on the Elbe*. In the inspiring opening sequence, the Russian army is seen approaching the Elbe, orderly, joyous soldiers mounted on gleaming tanks, each tank carrying a laurel wreath and a portrait of Stalin. Suddenly, we hear the corrupt, jerky strains of Yankee Doodle Dandy, and the camera swoops down on the opposite bank, where the unshaven behemoths who make up the American army are revealed staggering toward the river, soldiers stumbling drunkenly into the water. On the symbolically lowered bridge, the white-uniformed Russian colonel, upright as Gary Cooper, says, 'It's good to see the American army – even if it's on the last day of the war.' Then he passes his binoculars to his American counterpart, a tubby pig-eyed Lou Costello figure. The American colonel scowls, displeased to see his men fraternizing with the Russians. Suddenly, he grins slyly. 'You must admit,' he says, lowering the binoculars, 'that the Germans made excellent optical equipment.' The Russian colonel replies: 'These binoculars were made in Moscow, comrade.'

In the Russian zone, always seen by day, the Gary Cooper colonel has set up his headquarters in a modest farm house. Outside, his adorable orderly, a Ukrainian Andy Devine, cavorts with sandyhaired German kids, reciting Heine to them. But in the American zone, seen only by night, the obese, cigar-chomping American colonel has appropriated a castle. Loutish enlisted men parade enormous oil paintings before him, and the colonel chalks a big X on those he wants shipped home. All the while, I should add, he is on the long distance line to Wall Street, asking for quotations on Bavarian forest.

Recently, I have been reading John Clellon Holmes's *Nothing More To Declare,* a memoir which makes it plain that the ideas and idiom, even some of the people, prevalent in the Village during the Fifties were interchangeable with those in Paris. The truculent Legman, once a *Neurotica* editor, of whom he writes so generously, inevitably turned up in St. Germain des Prés to produce his definitive edition of filthy limericks on rag paper and, incidentally, to assure us gruffly that the novel was dead. Absolutely dead.

Even as in the Village, we were obsessed by the shared trivia and pop of our boyhood, seldom arguing about ideas, which would have made us feel self-conscious, stuffy, but instead going on and on about Fibber McGee's closet, Mandrake's enemies, Warner Brothers' character actors like Elisha Cook Jr., the Andrews Sisters, and the Katzenjammer Kids. To read about such sessions now in other people's novels or essays doesn't make for recognition so much as resentment at having one's past broadcast, played back as it were, a ready-to-wear past, which in retrospect was not peculiar to Paris but a Fifties commonplace.

At times it seems to me that what my generation of novelists does best, celebrating itself, is also discrediting. Too often, I think, it is we who are the fumblers, the misfits, *but unmistakably lovable,* intellectual heroes of our very own fictions, triumphant in our vengeful imaginations as we never were in actuality. Only a few contemporaries, say Brian Moore, live up to what I once took to be the novelist's primary moral responsibility, which is to be the loser's advocate. To tell us what it's like to be Judith Hearne. Or a pinched Irish school teacher. The majority tend to compose paeans of disguised praise of people very much like themselves. Taken to an extreme, the fictional guise is dropped and we are revealed cheering ourselves. And so George Plimpton is the pitcher and hero of *Out of My League* by George Plimpton. Norman Podhoretz, in *Making It,* is the protagonist of his own novel. And most recently, in *The Armies of the Night*, Norman Mailer writes about himself in the third person.

This is not to plead for a retreat to social realism or novels of protest, but simply to say that, as novelists, many of us are perhaps too easily bored, too self-regarding, and not sufficiently curious about mean lives, bland people. The unglamorous.

All at once, it was spring.
One day shopkeepers were wretched, waiters surly, concierges mean about taking messages, and the next, the glass windows encasing café terraces were removed everywhere, and Parisians were transmogrified: shopkeepers, waiters, concierges actually spoke in dulcet tones.

Afternoons we took to the Jardins du Luxembourg, lying on the grass and speculating about Duke Snider's arm, the essays in *The God That Failed*, Jersey Joe Walcott's age, whether Salinger's *The Catcher in the Rye* could be good *and* a Book-of-the-Month, how far Senator Joe McCarthy might go, was Calder Willingham over-rated, how much it might set us back to motorcycle to Seville, was Alger Hiss lying, why wasn't Nathaniel West more widely read, could Don Newcombe win thirty games, and was it disreputable of Max Brod to withhold Kafka's "Letter to My Father."

Piaf was big with us, as was Jacques Prévert's *Paroles,* the song *Les Feuilles mortes,* Trenet, and the films of Simone Signoret. Anything by Genet, or Samuel Beckett, was passed from hand to hand. I tried to read *La Nausée* in French, but stumbled and gave it up.

Early one Sunday morning in May, laying in a kitbag filled with wine, *paté*, hardboiled eggs, guiches and salamis and cold veal from the charcuterie, cheeses, a bottle of armagnac and baguettes, five of us squeezed into a battered Renault quatre-chevaux and set off for Chartres and the beaches of Normandy. 1952 it was, but we soon discovered that the rocky beaches were still littered with the debris of war. Approaching the coast we bumped drunkenly past shelled-out, crumbling buildings, VERBOTEN printed on one wall and ACHTUNG! on another. This moved us to incredulous laughter, evoking old Warner Brothers films and dimly recalled hit parade tunes. But, once on the beaches, we were sobered and silent. Incredibly thick pill boxes, split and shattered, had yet to be cleared away. Others, barely damaged, clearly showed scorch-marks. Staring into the dark pill boxes, through gun slits that were still intact, was chilling, even though gulls now squawked reassuringly overhead. Barefoot, our trousers rolled to the knees, we roamed the beaches, finding deep pits and empty shell cases here and there. As the tide receded, concrete teeth were revealed still aimed at the incoming tanks and landing craft. I stopped to retrieve a soldier's boot from a garland of sea weed. Slimy, soggy, already sea-green, I could still make out the bullet-hole in the toe.

Ikons.
We were not, it's worth noting, true adventurers, but followers of a romantic convention. A second *Aliyah*, so to speak. 'History has not quite repeated itself,' Brian Moore wrote in a review of *Exile's Return* for the *Spectator*. 'When one reads of the passionate, naïve manifestos in Malcolm Cowley's "literary odyssey of the 1920s," the high ambitions and the search for artistic values which sent the "lost generation" to Paris, one cannot help feeling a touch of envy. It would seem that the difference between the American artists' pilgrimage to Europe in the Twenties and in the Sixties is the difference between first love and the obligatory initial visit to a brothel.

'Moneyed by a grant from Fulbright, Guggenheim, or Ford, the American painter now goes to France for a holiday: he knows that the action is all in New York. Similarly, the young American writer abroad shows little interest in the prose experiments of Robbe-Grillet, Sarraute, and Simon; he tends to dismiss Britain's younger novelists and playwrights as boring social realists (*we finished with that stuff twenty years ago*), and as for Sartre, Beckett, Genet, or Ionesco, he has dug them already off-Broadway. It seems that American writers, in three short generations, have moved from the provincial (*we haven't yet produced any writing that could be called major*) to the parochial (*the only stuff worth reading nowadays is coming out of America*).'

Our group, in the Fifties, came sandwiched between, largely unmoneyed, except for those on the GI Bill, and certainly curious about French writing, especially Sartre, Camus, and, above all, Céline. We were also self-consciously aware of the Twenties. We knew the table at the Dôme that had been Hemingway's and made a point of eating at the restaurant on rue Monsieur le Prince where Joyce was reputed to have taken his dinner. Not me, but others regularly sipped tea with Alice Toklas. Raymond Duncan, swirling past in his toga, was a common, if absurd, sight. *Transition* still appeared fitfully.

Other connections with the Twenties were through the second-generation. David Burnett, one of the editors of *New-Story,* was the son of Whit Burnett and Martha Foley, who had brought out the original *Story*. My own first publication was in *Points*, a little magazine that was edited by Sinbad Vail, the son of Lawrence Vail and Peggy Guggenheim. It wasn't much of a magazine, and though Vail printed 4,000 copies of the first issue, he was only able to peddle 400. In the same issue as my original mawkish short story there was a better one by Brendan Behan, who was described as '27, Irish . . . Has been arrested several times for activities in the Irish Republican Army, which he joined in 1937, and in all has been sentenced to 17 years in gaol, has in fact served about 7 years in Borstal and Parkhurst Prison. Disapproves of English prison system. At present working as a housepainter on the State Railways.'

Among other little magazines current at the time there were *Id* and *Janus* ('An aristocrat by his individualism, a revolutionary against all societies,' wrote Daniel Mauroc, 'the homosexual is both the Jew and the Negro, the precursor and the unassimilable, the terrorist and the *raffiné*. . . .') and *Merlin,* edited by Trocchi, Richard Seaver, Logue, and John Coleman, who is now the *New Statesman*'s film critic. *Merlin*'s address, incidentally, was the English Bookshop, 42 rue de Seine, which had once belonged to Sylvia Beach.

In retrospect, I cannot recall that anybody, except Alan Temko, perhaps, was as yet writing fantasy or satire. Mostly, the stories we published were realistic and about home, be it Texas, Harlem, Brooklyn, or Denver. Possibly, just possibly, everything can be stripped down to a prosaic explanation. The cult of hashish, for instance, had a simple economic basis. It was easy to come by and cheap, far cheaper than scotch. Similarly, if a decade after our sojourn in Paris a number of us began to write what has since come to be branded black humour, it may well be that we were not so much inspired as driven to it by mechanics. After all, the writer who opts out of the mainstream of American experience, self-indulgently luxuriating in bohemia, the pleasure of like-minded souls, is also cutting himself off from his natural material, sacrificing his sense of social continuity; and so when we swung round to writing about contemporary America, we could only attack obliquely, shrewdly settling on a style that did not betray knowledge gaps of day to day experience.

For the most part, I moved with the *New-Story* bunch, David Burnett, Terry Southern, Mason Hoffenberg, Alan Temko, and others. One afternoon, Burnett told me, a new arrival from the States walked into the office and said, 'For ten thousand dollars, I will stop in front of a car on the Place Vendôme and say I did it because *New-Story* rejected one of my stories. Naturally, I'm willing to guarantee coverage in all the American newspapers.'

'But what if you're hurt?' he was asked.

'Don't worry about me, I'm a paraphrase artist.'

'A what?'

'I can take any story in *Collier's*, rewrite it, and sell it to the *Post*.'

New-Story, beset by financial difficulties from the very first issue, seldom able to fork out the promised two bucks a page to contributors or meet printer's bills, was eventually displaced by the more affluent *Paris Review*. But during its short and turbulent life *New-Story* was, I believe, the first magazine to publish Jean Genet in English. Once, browsing at George Whitman's hole-in-the-wall bookshop near Notre-Dame, where Bernard Frechtman's translation of *Our Lady of the Flowers* was prominently displayed, I overheard an exasperated Whitman explain to a camera-laden American matron, 'No, no, it's not the same Genet as writes for the *New Yorker*.'

Possibly, the most memorable of all the little magazines was the French publication, *Ur, Cahiers Pour Un Dictat Culturel*. *Ur* was edited by Jean-Isador Isou, embattled author of *A Reply To Karl Marx*, a slender riposte hawked by gorgeous girls in blue jeans to tourists at right bank cafés – tourists under the tantalizing illusion that they were buying the hot stuff.

Ur was a platform for the Letterists, who believed that all the arts were dead and could only be resurrected by a synthesis of their collective absurdities. This, like anything else that was seemingly new or outrageous, appealed to us. And so Friday nights, our pockets stuffed with oranges and apples, pitching cores into the Seine, scuffling, singing *Adon Olam*, we passed under the shadows of Notre Dame and made our way to a café on the Ile St. Louis to listen to Isador Isou and others read poems composed of grunts and cries, incoherent arrangements of letters, set to an anti-musical background of vacuum cleaners, drills, car horns, and train whistles. We listened, rubbing our jaws, nodding, looking pensive.

– *Ça, alors.*

– *Je m'en fous.*

– *Azoi*, Ginsberg. *Azoi.*

Ginsberg was the first to go home. I asked him to see my father and tell him how hard up I was.

'Sometimes,' Ginsberg told him, 'your son sits up all night in his cold room, writing.'

'And what does he do all day?'

Crack peanuts on the terrace of the Café Royale. Ruminate over the baseball scores in the *Herald-Tribune*.

We were all, as Hemingway once said, at the right age. Everybody was talented. Special. Nobody had money. (Except of course Art Buchwald, the most openly envied ex-GI in Paris. Buchwald, who had not yet emerged as a humourist, had cunningly solved two problems at once, food and money, inaugurating a restaurant column in the *Herald-Tribune*.) We were all trying to write or paint and so there was always the hope, it's true, of a publisher's advance or a contract with a gallery. There was also the national lottery. There was, too, the glorious dream that today you would run into the fabled lady senator from the United States who was reputed to come over every summer and, as she put it, invest in the artistic future of five or six promising, creative youngsters. She would give you a thousand dollars, more sometimes, no strings attached. But I never met her. I was reminded of the days when as a kid in Montreal I was never without a Wrigley's chewing gum wrapper, because of that magic man who could pop up anywhere, stop you, and ask for a wrapper. If you had one with you, he gave you a dollar. Some days, they said, he handed out as much as fifty dollars. I never met him, either.

Immediately before Christmas, however, one of my uncles sent me money. I had written to him, quoting Auden, Kierkegaard, *The Book of Changes,* Maimonides, and Dylan Thomas, explaining we must love one another or die. 'I can hear that sort of crap,' he wrote back, 'any Sunday morning on the Manischewitz Hour,' but a cheque for a hundred dollars was enclosed, and I instantly decided to go to Cambridge for the holidays.

Stringent rationing – goose eggs, a toe-nail size chunk of meat a week – was still the depressing rule in England and, as I had old friends in Cambridge, I arrived laden with foodstuffs, my raincoat sagging with contraband steaks and packages of butter. A friend of a friend took me along to sip sherry with E. M. Forster at his rooms in King's College.

Forster immediately unnerved me by asking what I thought of F. Scott Fitzgerald's work.

Feebly, I replied I thought very highly of it indeed.

Forster then remarked that he generally asked visiting young Americans what they felt about Fitzgerald, whose high reputation baffled him. Forster said that though Fitzgerald unfailingly chose the most lyrical titles for his novels, the works themselves seemed to him to be without especial merit.

Unaccustomed to sherry, intimidated by Forster, who in fact couldn't have been more kind or gentle, I stupidly knocked back my sherry in one gulp, like a synagogue schnapps, whilst the others sipped theirs decorously. Forster waved for my glass to be refilled and then inquired without the least condescension about the progress of my work. Embarrassed, I hastily changed the subject.

'And what,' he asked, 'do you make of Angus's first novel?'

Angus being Angus Wilson and the novel, *Hemlock and After*.

'I haven't read it yet,' I lied, terrified lest I made a fool of myself.

I left Forster a copy of Nelson Algren's *The Man With The Golden Arm*, which I had just read and enormously admired. A few days later the novel was returned to me with a note I didn't keep, and so quote from memory. He had only read as far as page 120 in Algren's novel, Forster wrote. It had less vomit than the last American novel he had read, but ...

At the time, I was told that the American novel Forster found most interesting was Willard Motley's *Knock On Any Door*.

Cambridge, E. M. Forster, was a mistake; it made me despair for me and my friends and our shared literary pretensions. In the rooms I visited at King's, St. Mary's, and Pembroke, gowned young men were wading through the entire *Faerie*

Queene, they had absorbed *Beowulf*, Chaucer, and were clearly heirs to the tradition. All at once, it seemed outlandish, a grandiose *chutzpah*, that we, street corner bohemians, kibbitzers, still swapping horror stories about our abominable Yiddish mommas, should even presume to write. Confirmation, if it were needed, was provided by John Lehmann, who returned my first attempt at a sub-Céline novel with a printed rejection slip.

'Hi, keed,' my brother wrote. 'How are things in Gay Paree?', and there followed a list of the latest YMHA basketball scores.

Things in Gay Paree were uncommonly lousy. I had contracted scurvy, of all things, from not eating sufficient fruit or vegetables. The money began to run out. Come midnight, come thirst, I used to search for my affluent friend, Armstrong, who was then putting me up in his apartment in Étoile. I would seek out Armstrong in the homosexual pits of St. Germain and Montparnasse. The Montana, the Fiacre, l'Abbaye, the Reine Blanche. If Armstrong was sweetening up a butch, I would slip in and out again discreetly, but if Armstrong was alone, alone and sodden, he would comfort me with cognacs and ham rolls and take me home in a taxi.

Enormous, rosycheeked, raisineyed Armstrong was addicted to acquired Yiddishisms. He'd say, 'Oy, bless my little. I don't known why I go there, Mottel.'

'Uh huh.'

'Did you catch the old queen at the bar?'

'I'm still hungry. What about you?'

'*Zut.*'

'You know, I've never eaten at Les Halles. All this time in Paris...'

'I don't care a tit if you ever eat at Les Halles. We're going home, you scheming *yenta*.'

Armstrong and I had sat next to each other in Political Science 101 at Sir George Williams College. SYSTEMS OF GOVERNMENT, the professor wrote on the blackboard,

a. monarchy   c. democracy
b. totalitarianism   d. others

Canada is a ―――――――――

Armstrong passed me a note. 'A Presbyterian twat.'

At Sir George, Armstrong had taken out the most desirable girls, but I could never make out. The girls I longed for longed for the basketball players or charmers like Armstrong and the only one who would tolerate me had been the sort who read Penguins on streetcars or were above using make-up. Or played the accordion at parties, singing about Joe Hill and *Los Quatro Générales*. Or demonstrated. Then, two years ago, Armstrong had tossed up everything to come to Paris and study acting. Now he no longer put up with girls and had become an unstoppable young executive in a major advertising company. 'I would only have made a mediocre actor,' he was fond of saying to me as I sat amidst my rejection slips.

Once more I was able to wangle money from home, three hundred dollars, and this time I ventured south for the summer, to Haut-de-Cagnes. Here I first encountered American and British expatriates of the Twenties, shadowy remittance men, coupon-clippers, who painted a bit, sculpted some, and wrote from time to time. An instructive but shattering look, I feared, at my future prospects. Above all, the expatriates drank prodigiously. Twenties flotsam, whose languid, self-indulgent bickering, party-crammed life in the Alpes-Maritimes had been disrupted only by World War II.

Bit players of a bygone age, they persisted in continuing as if it were still burgeoning, supplying the *Nice-Matin*, for instance, with guest lists of their lawn parties; and carrying on as if Cyril Connelly's first novel, *The Rockpool*, were a present scandal. 'He was only here for three weeks altogether, don't you know,' a colonel told me.

'I'm only *very* thinly disguised in it,' a lady said haughtily.

Extremely early one morning I rolled out of bed in response to a knock on the door. It was Mr. Soon.

'I have just seen the sun coming up over the Mediterranean,' he said.

In spite of the heat, Mr. Soon wore a crushed greasy raincoat. Terry Southern, if I remember correctly, had given it to him. He had also thoughtfully provided him with my address.

'Won't you come in?' I asked.

'Not yet. I am going to walk on the Promenade des Anglais.'

'You might as well leave your coat here, then.'

'But it would be inelegant to walk on the Promenade in Nice without a coat, don't you think?'

Mr. Soon returned late in the afternoon and I took him to Jimmy's Bar, on the brim of the steep grey hill of Haut-de-Cagnes.

'It reminds me most of California here,' Mr. Soon said.

'But I had no idea you had ever been to California.'

'No. Never. Have you?'

I watched, indeed, soon everyone on the terrace turned to stare, as Mr. Soon, his beard a filthy tangle, reached absently into his pocket for a magnifying glass, held it to the sun, and lit a Gauloise. Mr. Soon, who spoke several languages, including Chinese, imperfectly, was evasive whenever we asked him where he had been born in this his twenty-third reincarnation. We put him down for Russian, but when I brought him along to Marushka's she insisted that he spoke the language ineptly.

Marushka, now in her sixties, had lived in Cagnes for years. Modigliani had written a sonnet to her and she could recall the night Isadora had danced in the square. Marushka was not impressed by Mr. Soon. 'He's a German,' she said, as if it was quite the nastiest thing she could think of.

I took Mr. Soon home with me and made up a bed for him on the floor, only to be awakened at two a.m. because all the lights had been turned on. Mr. Soon sat at my table, writing, with one of my books, *The Guide For The Perplexed*, by his side. 'I am copying out the table of contents,' he said.

'But what on earth for?'

'It is a very interesting table of contents, don't you think?'

A week later Mr. Soon was still with me. One afternoon he caught me hunting mosquitoes with a rolled newspaper and subjected me to a long, melancholy lecture on the holy nature of all living things. Infuriated, I said, 'Maybe *I* was a mosquito in a previous incarnation, eh?'

'No. You were a Persian Prince.'

'What makes you say that?' I asked, immensely pleased.

'Let us go to Jimmy's. It is so interesting to sit there and contemplate, don't you think?'

I was driven to writing myself a letter and opening it while Mr. Soon and I sat at the breakfast table. 'Some friends of mine are coming down from Paris the day after tomorrow. I'd quite forgotten I had invited them to stay with me.'

'Very interesting. How long will they be staying?'

'There's no saying.'

'I can stay at the Tarzan Camping and return when they are gone.'

We began to sell things. Typewriters, books, wristwatches. When we all seemed to have reached bottom, when our credit was no longer good anywhere, something turned up. An ex-GI, Seymour, who ran a tourist office in Nice called SEE-MOR TOURS, became casting director for extra parts in films and we all got jobs for ten dollars a day.

Once more, Armstrong tolerated me in his Paris flat. One night, in the Montana, Armstrong introduced me to an elegant group of people at his table, including the Countess Louise. The next morning he informed me, 'Louise, um, thinks you're cute, boychick. She's just dumped Jacques and she's looking for another banana.'

Armstrong went on to explain that if I were satisfactory I would have a studio in Louise's flat and an allowance of one hundred thousand francs monthly.

'And what do I have to do to earn all that?'

'Oy-vey. There's nothing like a Jewish childhood. Don't be so provincial.'

Louise was a thin wizened lady in her forties. Glittering earrings dripped from her ears and icy rings swelled on the fingers of either hand. 'It would only be once a week,' Armstrong said. 'She'd take you to first nights at the opera and all the best restaurants. Wouldn't you like that?'

'Go to hell.'

'You're invited to her place for drinks on Thursday. I'd better buy you some clothes first.'

On Thursday I sat in the sun at the Mabillion consuming beer after beer before I risked the trip to the Countess's flat. I hadn't felt as jumpy or been so thoroughly bright and scrubbed from the skin out since my bar-mitzvah. A butler took my coat. The hall walls were painted scarlet and embedded with precious stones. I was led into the drawing room where a nude study of a younger Louise, who had used to be a patroness of surrealists, hung in a lighted alcove. Spiders and bugs fed on the Countess's ash-grey bosom. I heard laughter and voices from another room. Finally a light-footed American in a black antelope jacket drifted into the drawing room. 'Louise is receiving in the bedroom,' he said.

Possibly, I thought, I'm one of many candidates. I stalked anxiously round an aviary of stuffed tropical fowl. Leaning against the mantelpiece, I knocked over an antique gun.

'Oh, dear.' The young American retrieved it gently. 'This,' he said, 'is the gun Verlaine used in his duel with Rimbaud.'

At last Louise was washed into the room on a froth of beautiful boys and girls. She took my hand and pressed it. 'Well, hullo,' I said.

We sped off in two black Jaguars to a private party for Cocteau. All the bright young people, except me, had some accomplishment behind them. They chatted breezily about their publishers and producers and agents. Eventually one of them turned to me, offering a smile. 'You're Louise's little Canadian, aren't you?'

'That's the ticket.'

Louise asked me about Montreal.

'After Paris,' I said, swaying drunkenly, 'it's the world's largest French-speaking city.'

The American in the black antelope jacket joined me at the bar, clapping me on the shoulder. 'Louise will be very good to you,' he said.

Azoi.

'We all adore her.'

Suddenly Louise was with us. 'But you must meet Cocteau,' she said.

I was directed to a queue awaiting presentation. Cocteau wore a suede windbreaker. The three young men ahead of me, one of them a sailor, kissed him on both cheeks as they were introduced. Feeling foolish, I offered him my hand and then returned to the bar and had another whisky, and yet another, before I noticed that all my group, including my Countess, had gone, leaving me behind.

Armstrong was not pleased with me, but then he was a troubled man. His secretary, a randy little bit from Guildford, an ex-India Army man's daughter, was eager for him, and Armstrong, intimidated, had gone so far as to fondle her breasts at the office. 'If I don't screw the bitch,' he said to me, 'she'll say I'm queer. Oy, my poor *tuchus.*'

Armstrong's day-to-day existence was fraught with horrors. Obese, he remained a compulsive eater. Terrified of blackmailers and police *provocateurs,* he was still driven to cruising Piccadilly and Leicester Square on trips to London. Every day he met with accountants and salesmen, pinched men in shiny office suits who delighted in vicious jokes about queers, and Armstrong felt compelled to prove himself the most ferocious queer-baiter of them all.

'Maybe I should marry Betty. She wants to. Well, boychick?'

In the bathroom, I looked up to see black net bikini underwear dripping from a line over the tub. Armstrong pounded on the door. 'We could have kids,' he said.

The medicine cabinet was laden with deodorants and sweetening sprays and rolls of absorbent cotton and Vaseline jars.

'I'm capable, you know.'

A few nights later Armstrong brought a British boy home. A painter, a taschist. 'Oy, Mottel,' he said, easing me out of the flat. '*Gevalt,* old chap.'

The next morning I stumbled into the bathroom, coming sharply awake when I saw a red rose floating in the toilet bowl.

After Armstrong had left for work, the painter, a tall fastidious boy with flaxen hair, joined me at the breakfast table. He misunderstood my frostiness. 'I wouldn't be staying here,' he assured me, 'but Richard said your relationship is platonic.'

I looked up indignantly from my newspaper, briefly startled, then smiled and said, 'Well, you see I could never take him home and introduce him to my family. He's not Jewish.'

Two weeks later my father sent me enough money for a ticket home and, regretfully, I went to the steamship office at l'Opéra. An advertisement in the window read:

> 'liked Lisbon, loved Tahiti. But when it comes to
> getting the feel of the sea ...'
> give me the crashing waves and rugged rocks
> give me the gulls and nets and men and boats
> give me the harbours and homes and spires and quays
> GIVE ME NEW BRUNSWICK
> CANADA

I had been away two years.

GORDON CRAIG

Let me say at once that I hadn't the foggiest idea who Edward Gordon Craig was when I met him in 1952. The first time I saw Craig he was sitting in the sun at a café table on the square in Vence, playing patience. He wore, as was his habit, a white linen suit, the jacket tumbling to his knees, and a floppy-brimmed straw hat. My friend Jean-Luc introduced me. 'Are you an artist?' Craig demanded immediately.

'Well,' I said, fumbling, 'I'm trying to write. I . . .'

'*Good*. I'm working on my memoirs.'

A British publisher had commissioned the work, but Craig was now on his third manuscript volume and had not yet reached the literary age of nineteen. The publisher, alarmed, had offered to buy all Craig's personal papers and commission somebody else to write the biography. 'But would you let them have Isadora's love letters?' he asked me.

Isadora, I grasped, was Isadora Duncan. Before I could reply, a man just returned from Vallauris came to the table. He brought regards from Picasso.

'I *should* visit him,' Craig said. 'It would be very good publicity for me to have my picture taken with him now. Have you a car?'

'Sorry,' I said.

Suddenly Craig slammed his cane across the table, a startling gesture, and indicated the initials 'H.I.' engraved on the gold band round the top. 'This was the master's,' he said. 'Irving always had them imported. South American malacca.'

We called for another round of beer.

'A young man was here yesterday to take pictures of me,' Craig said. Then he paused, his eyes narrowed, and he studied the length of his cane. Just as he felt our attention had begun to wander, he leaned forward, a conspirator, and added, 'He says he's my son.'

I looked astonished. Obviously, this pleased Craig enormously. He smiled. 'I don't think he's my son,' he said. 'Pity you haven't got a car.'

Craig asked me, as I was a writer, if I could please explain why so many people came to take photographs of him and none was ever published. I couldn't tell him they were being held for his obituary notices. 'I really don't know,' I said.

Jean-Luc and I lived in Tourrettes-sur-loup, some four miles further up the winding mountain road, and we started back together, cutting through the hot, dusty olive groves. Jean-Luc, a playwright himself, told me that Craig was a theatrical genius. A neglected genius. He had begun his career as an actor in Henry Irving's Lyceum Theatre in 1889. When he was still young and unknown, W. B. Yeats used to come to see him in his room off the Euston Road. In 1904 he prepared designs for plays and masques for the Lessing Theatre in Berlin. Later he worked with Eleonora Duse and Isadora Duncan. At a public dinner given in his honour in London in 1911, by which time Craig was an acknowledged leader in the European theatre, celebrated for his theory (*The Art of the Theatre,* 1905; *On the Art of the Theatre,* 1911) as well as his revolutionary designs, W. B. Yeats said, 'A great age is an age which employs its men of genius; a poor age is an age which has no use for them. This age finds it difficult to employ men of genius like Mr. Craig.' Craig first went to Russia in 1905, where he met Stanislavsky and Fokine. He returned to Russia in 1910, at the invitation of Stanislavsky, to design a production of *Hamlet*.

Craig had promised to visit us that night. He had a friend in Tourrettes, a Colonel Hiller.

The mediaeval village of Tourrettes-sur-loup, jutting natural as rock over a bony ravine, is in the foothills of the Alpes-Maritimes behind Nice. Our gritty little colony of foreigners there, in 1952, included Jean-Luc and his mistress; an ambitious Australian potter, his wife and child; a Viennese abstract painter; a would-be novelist from Texas who, to the unending delight of the boule players, was given to strolling across the village square in cowboy boots; and in the villas strewn over the surrounding hills some twenties' flotsam, a wash of retired British army and colonial service officers who spluttered into Tourrettes once a week in ancient cars to have their wine casks refilled.

Craig, to our surprise, arrived on the six-fifteen bus. He looked around, briefly puzzled, a white rug slung over his shoulder. Then, recognizing us at a café table on the square, he waved his arms triumphantly, hooted, and scampered over to join us. He was eighty years old then. His mother, Ellen Terry, had died at the age of eighty-one, and Craig believed he was doomed to follow her. 'She appeared at the foot of my bed in a dream last night,' he said. 'She often does, you know.'

We asked him about his trip to Russia after the revolution.

'They're the most shocking prudes, you know. They were scandalized because my secretary was pregnant.' He told us that the best *King Lear* he had ever seen had been performed by the Habima in Moscow. 'The authorities wanted me to say theatre had improved since the revolution, but they couldn't trick me . . .'

It soon became obvious that Craig's world was filled with two sorts of people: artists and non-artists. The artists, ourselves included, were an adorable band of gypsies united against bad taste, though always willing to accept the protection of any politician or tycoon, be they fascist, communist, or what have you.

Craig talked endlessly, demonstratively impatient, even rude, when any of the others at the table even touched briefly on a subject that did not include him. He told us that when he had been living in Florence, where, from 1908 to 1929, he had edited, published and, under various pseudonyms, written *The Mask,* Mussolini had summoned him to an interview. Craig had assumed the dictator was going to build him a theatre and elaborated on the sort he wanted.

'But what did you think of Mussolini?' I interrupted.

'He had the most wonderful sense of theatre,' Craig said.

He went on to describe, acting out both parts, how he had entered Mussolini's office and had seen him sitting behind an enormous desk at the end of a wide sweep of marble floor. Craig had approached, books under his arm, conscious of his footsteps resounding on the marble, the dictator's glare, and the humiliating distance he still had to cover. 'Mussolini,' he said, 'picked up my book of sketches, flipped through them upside down, and muttered something to an advisor. He had thought I was an architect,' Craig said, slamming his fist against the table. 'No theatre.'

Midnight came, it passed, and Craig was still with us. It had grown chilly, the last bus had gone. We began to whisper among ourselves. Shouldn't he be in bed? Two o'clock. The café closed and still Craig's large laughter filled the square. Whenever our attention faltered – the truth was *we* were getting tired – Craig banged the master's cane against the table to emphasize a point. At last a Hillman Minx pulled up across the square and Craig leaped to his feet. 'Ah. My mistress!' He gathered his things together and hurried off. Before climbing into the car, however, he assured us, 'Be back tomorrow morning.'

He came on the first bus and sent a boy round to knock on our doors and wake us. Bleary-eyed, we gathered again.

Craig took us up, I think, because he was generally in the

company of fading retired people. A condition he did not enjoy. He was, at the time, being shunted from one *pension* to another. Craig was a foul-tempered, demanding guest, a blight innkeepers shared, like the mistral.

Craig had brought an enormous collection of recent photographs of himself. 'I want you to sift through them carefully, very carefully,' he said, 'and select the best.' As he felt we ought to discuss the charms of each study it proved a lengthy chore. Afterwards, however, he signed photographs – 'Affectionately, E.G.C.' – for each of us.

Craig never came to Tourrettes empty-handed; he always had something to show us. Once he appeared with a folio of precious cartoons and other items by Beerbohm. There was a drawing of the young handsome Craig leaping over a banquet table and – a jarringly childish prank, this – a double-page spread of photographs of company directors clipped from the *Illustrated London News* and altered by Beerbohm. The eyes of some had been crossed, a moustache or side-whiskers had been added to others, but all had been made to appear uniformly ridiculous. Beerbohm had also added one puncturing sentence to the potted biography of each director that appeared under the photographs. Beerbohm was, at the time, still resident in Rapallo. The B.B.C. had invited several old friends to broadcast tributes to him on his eightieth birthday. The gist of Craig's memoir was, 'Max is eighty, *I'm going on eighty-one*, and nobody has paid tribute to me . . .'

Another day Craig brought me copies of several of his books. There were pencilled comments in all of them. To begin with, in the book about Henry Irving, there was a list of titles of Craig's previous books. Beside each title he had calculated in pencil how much each book had earned for him. All the sums were added up at the bottom and divided by the actual number of books to give him the average earnings of each one. Below, there was a notation in pencil saying, 'What shoddy paper this book has been printed on. Will it have turned to dust in fifty years? E.G.C., Florence, 192-.' All

Craig's notes were initialled, dated, and precisely placed (on the road to Florence, Vence, et cetera). As soon as page eleven in a book ostensibly about Irving, Craig gives us a description of himself crossing the Atlantic with Ellen Terry. 'If anybody is curious to see what I looked like at that time,' he writes, 'they will find me in a group photographed on board the "Arizona," in which we came back from America in 1885.' A pencilled footnote below further informs us, giving the date, that the photograph appeared in the New York *Herald-Tribune*. I should add that Craig was, at the time, all of thirteen years old. Elsewhere, various footnotes were pencilled in *Henry Irving* over a span of thirty years. When he produced his first play in London, Craig recounts in the book, somebody with an outlandish feminine name wrote to say how inordinately bad the production was. 'Could this letter,' a pencilled note reads, 'have been from G.B.S. in disguise?' Another note, written years later, reads, 'It must have been.' In another passage, Craig suggests in a printed footnote that if anyone wanted to know what he and his friends were up to in the theatre they might read books by Allardyce Nicoll and Glenn Hughes. A footnote reflects on how much in royalties this recommendation must have earned the two men and yet they never wrote to thank Craig. A further note, written some years later, observes that you'd think they would have written by this time. The final note, written in Vence, says, 'They still haven't written.'

When I turned to another page of the book, a typewritten letter fell out. It was written in English, to Craig, from Sergei Eisenstein. Eisenstein wrote to say how much he had enjoyed their last meeting in Paris and how he was looking forward to seeing Craig again in Moscow.

Craig told me, 'Oh yes, Eisenstein. He studied my book on Irving like a Bible. He had made elaborate notes and he questioned me all night about Irving's technique.'

Craig never threw anything out. He still retained all the sketches he had ever made when he had used to go to the music halls in London as a youth. His friend, Colonel Hiller, told me that several years earlier the Victoria and Albert Museum in London had made Craig a considerable offer for all his letters, manuscripts, woodcuts, and memorabilia, but he had turned them down. Later he was to sell everything to the Bibliothèque Nationale in Paris.

He was, I remember, often disturbed by newspaper accounts that referred to him as the late Edward Gordon Craig. One day he came to Tourrettes, infuriated. A press agent's story in the Paris edition of the *Herald-Tribune* had described an encounter between Orson Welles and Craig in the American Express. Welles, according to the story, bowed deeply and said, 'Master. My Master.'

'Very flattering, I suppose,' Craig said, 'but I never met Welles.'

I left Tourrettes a week later and my last glimpse of Craig, from the bus, was on the square in Vence. He was playing patience. He looked bored and eager for an interruption.

When I returned to Tourrettes four years later, in 1956, the first person I saw there was Craig. He sat at the café on the square, seemingly unchanged, talking to Colonel Hiller. I did not expect him to recognize me and he didn't. I had to introduce myself again. 'I've brought you regards,' I said.

'Who?' he said, cupping an ear.

'I've been asked to bring you regards from a friend of yours.'

'A gift! You've brought me a gift!'

'Regards,' I said, flushing.

'REGARDS,' Colonel Hiller shouted. 'NOT A GIFT.'

'Oh,' Craig said, his head dropping, dejected.

Since I had last seen him, Craig had enjoyed a revival of sorts. Many of his early books had been re-issued and he was much better off, financially, than he had been in 1952. He had also moved from Vence to an inn on the edge of the Tourrettes ravine. The inn was run by a retired French army officer, an opium-eater, and his teenage Arab boy friend. Craig adored sitting on the terrace, talking about art and artists, his white hair flowing in the wind and his chin resting on H.I.'s cane.

One of Edward Gordon Craig's dearest ambitions had still not been realized – he hadn't been knighted.

In the final chapter of *Henry Irving,* after Craig has, so to speak, finished the book, the master's spirit appears in his study.

'You must not think I exaggerate,' Craig wrote. 'I was alone; the wind, 'tis true, was howling down the valley outside my house – how it howwwled – yet all was cosy and well-lit in my room – nothing dusky, nothing weird: yet there – there stood Irving.'

After man and ghost had discoursed for a while, Irving observed, 'Er – yes: by the bye, I see you have been knighted, my boy – very good – very good.'

Craig protested vehemently that he had not been knighted.

'Not knighted – but it's in the papers!'

'No, Henry... that was somebody else... an Ernest Gordon Craig.'

'Ah! Ernest – Ernest,' repeated Irving – 'Wilde pointed to the er-r – importance of that...'

Craig was included in the Queen's Honours List in 1956 and his Companion of Honour (C.H.) was presented to him by the British consul in Nice. At the small party for Craig, I'm told the consul began to recite a verse of Browning.

'Byron?' Craig interrupted. 'Is that Byron?'

'BROWNING!'

'I don't care for Browning.'

One day during that last summer in Tourrettes an eager young off-Broadway producer in Bermuda shorts turned up on the square. 'You mean to say Craig is still alive?' he said.

'There he is now.'

The producer took Craig to dinner, and he suggested, his manner breathless, that the old man might do a few sketches for his next production. Craig refused. But the last time I saw

Craig the flabby young man was at his elbow. 'Why don't we drive down to see Picasso?'

'Not today,' Craig said, wearily.

BOND

Commander James Bond, CMG, RNVR, springs from a long and undoubtedly loyal line of secret service agents and clubland heroes, including William Le Queux's incomparable Duckworth Drew.

> Before I could utter ought save a muffled curse, I was flung head first into an empty piano case, the heavy lid of which was instantly closed on me . . . I had been tricked!

Sapper's Bulldog Drummond. And John Buchan's Richard Hannay.

> He began to snort now and his breath came heavily. 'You infernal cad,' I said in good round English. 'I'm going to knock the stuffing out of you,' but he didn't understand what I was saying.

There have been thirteen Bond novels in all, the first coming in 1953, the others appearing at yearly intervals until 1965, after Ian Fleming's fatal heart attack. On his initial appearance in *Casino Royale*, James Bond was thirty-five years old, an age he has more or less maintained over the years. He is some six foot tall, with a lean bronzed face vaguely reminiscent of Hoagy Carmichael, a ruthless set to his mouth, and cold grey-blue eyes with a hint of anger in them. When Bond was eleven years old his parents, Andrew Bond of Glencoe, Scotland, and Monique Delacroiz of the canton of Vaud, Switzerland, were killed in a climbing accident; and so Bond was put in the care of his aunt, Miss Charmian Bond of Pett Bottom, Kent. At the age of twelve, he was sent off to Eton, wherefrom he was removed after two halves, as a result of some alleged trouble with one of the boys' maids. From Eton he went on to Fettes, his father's school. Here Bond flourished as a lightweight boxing champion and judo expert. In 1941, claiming to be nineteen years old, he entered the Ministry of Defence, where he soon became a lieutenant in the Special Branch of the RNVR, reaching the rank of commander by the war's end. In 1954, Bond was awarded a CMG, but nine years later he spurned a knighthood. He has been married once, in 1962, to Tracy, the Corsican countess Teresa di Vicenzo, daughter of the chief of the Union Corsa, Marc-Ange Draco. Tracy was murdered by Stavro Blofeld two hours after the wedding.

In 1955, Bond earned £1,500 a year and had a thousand free of tax on his own. He had a small but comfortable flat off the King's Road, an elderly Scottish housekeeper (a treasure called May) and a 1930 4½ litre Bentley coupé, supercharged, which he kept expertly tuned. In the evenings Bond played cards at Crockford's or made love 'with rather cold passion, to one of three similarly disposed married women,' and on the weekends he played golf for high stakes at one of the clubs near London.

In the first Bond novel, *Casino Royale*, Bond confides to Mathis, his colleague from the Deuxième Bureau, that in the previous few years he has killed two villains, a Japanese cipher expert and a Norwegian agent who was doubling for the Germans. For these two jobs, he was awarded a double 0 number in the Secret Service, which prefix gave him a licence to kill. Of late, however, he has begun to have qualms. This country-right-or-wrong business, he complains, is getting a little out of date. 'History is moving pretty quickly these days and the heroes and villains keep changing parts.' Finally, Mathis reassures Bond, explaining that there are still many villains seeking to destroy him and the England he loves. '... M will tell you about them.... There's still plenty to do. And you'll do it.... Surround yourself with human beings, my dear James. They are easier to fight for than principles.'

Bond next agonizes over his double 0 prefix in the opening pages of *Goldfinger*, reacting to a dirty assignment.

> ... What in the hell was he doing, glooming about the Mexican, this capungo who had been sent to kill him? It had been kill or get killed. Anyway, people were killing other people all the time, all over the world.... How many people, for instance, were involved in manufacturing H-bombs, from the miners who mined uranium to the shareholders who owned the mining shares?

Bond experiences another crisis (*For Your Eyes Only*) when M recruits him for an act of personal vengeance. To kill Von Hammerstein, 'who had operated the law of the jungle on two defenceless old people,' friends of M's. To begin with, Bond is sanguine. 'I would not hesitate for a minute, sir. If foreign gangsters find they can get away with this kind of thing they'll decide the English are as soft as some other people seem to think we are. This is a case for rough justice – an eye for an eye.' But once confronted with the villain in his camp,

> Bond did not like what he was going to do, and all the way from England he had to keep reminding himself ... Von Hammerstein and his gunmen were particularly dreadful men whom many people around the world would probably be very glad to destroy ... out of private revenge. But for Bond it was different. He had no personal

motives against them. *This was merely his job – as it was the job of a pest control officer to kill rats. He was the public executioner appointed by M to represent the community. . . .* (Emphasis mine)

Bond is not so much an anti-American, as condescending. Contemplating two American gangsters at the Saratoga race track, in *Diamonds Are Forever,* he wonders what these people amount to, set beside '. . . the people in his own Service – the double-firsts, the gay soldiers of fortune, the men who count life well lost for a thousand a year,' incidentally cutting his salary by a third since *Casino Royale*. Compared with such men, Bond decides, the gangsters 'were just teen-age pillow-fantasies.' But then, though he professes to enormously admire Allen Dulles, J. Edgar Hoover, and his CIA sidekick in many an adventure, Felix Leiter, he is not uncritical of a country where a fastidious man can't eat a boiled egg. When the villain in *The Hildebrand Rarity*, the coarse American millionaire, Milton Krest, put down England, arguing, nowadays there were only three powers – America, Russia, and China, 'That was the big poker game and no other country had either the chips or the cards to come into it,' – Bond replies (shatteringly, we are led to believe), 'Your argument reminds me of a rather sharp aphorism I once heard about America. . . . It's to the effect that America has progressed from infancy to senility without having passed through a period of maturity.'

Reflecting on the Russian *pysche,* in *From Russia With Love,* Bond says,

'. . . They simply don't understand the carrot. Only the stick has any effect. Basically they're masochists. They love the knout. That's why they were so happy under Stalin. He gave it to them. I'm not sure how they're going to react to the scraps of carrot they're being fed by Khrushchev and Co. As for England, the trouble today is that carrots for all are the fashion. At home and abroad. We don't show teeth any more – only gums.'

While Bond risks his neck abroad, a gay soldier of fortune and pest control officer, ungrateful England continues to deteriorate.

> James Bond slung his suitcase into the back of the old chocolate-brown Austin taxi and climbed into the front seat beside the foxy, pimpled young man in the black leather windcheater. The young man took a comb out of his breast pocket, ran it carefully through both sides of his duck-tail haircut, put the comb back into his pocket, then leaned forward and pressed the self-starter. The play with the comb, Bond guessed, was to assert to Bond that the driver was really only taking him and his money as a favour. It was typical of the cheap self-assertiveness of young labour since the war. This youth, thought Bond, makes about twenty pounds a week, despises his parents and would like to be Tommy Steele. It's not his fault. He was born into the buyers' market of the Welfare State and into the age of atomic bombs and space flight. For him life is empty and meaningless.

Duckworth Drew, Drummond, Hannay, carried with them on their adventures abroad an innate conviction of the British gentleman's superiority in all matters, a mystique acknowledged by wogs everywhere. Not so James Bond, who in his penultimate adventure, *You Only Live Twice,* must sit through the humiliating criticism of Tiger Tanaka, Head of the Japanese Secret Service.

> 'Bondo-san, I will now be blunt with you. . . . it is a sad fact that I, and many of us in positions of authority in Japan, have formed an unsatisfactory opinion about the British people since the war. You have not only lost a great Empire, you have seemed almost anxious to throw it away. . . . when you apparently sought to arrest this slide into impotence at Suez, you succeeded only in stage-managing one of the most pitiful bungles in the history

53

of the world. . . . Furthermore, your governments have shown themselves successively incapable of ruling and have handed over effective control of the country to the trade unions, who appear to be dedicated to the principle of doing less and less work for more money. This featherbedding, this shirking of an honest day's work, is sapping at ever-increasing speed the moral fibre of the British, a quality the world once so much admired. In its place we now see a vacuous, aimless horde of seekers after pleasure – gambling at the pools and bingo, whining at the weather and the declining fortunes of the country, and wallowing nostalgically in gossip about the doings of the Royal Family and your so-called aristocracy in the pages of the most debased newspapers in the world.'

Richard Hannay, to be sure, would have knocked the stuffing out of just such a jabbering Jap. Hannay, in his thumping, roseate time, could boast that in peace and war, by God, there was nothing to beat the British Secret Service, but poor James Bond, after Commander Crabbe, after Burgess and Maclean, after Kim Philby, could not make the same claim without appearing ludicrous even to himself.

If once British commanders sailed forth to jauntily plant the flag here, there, and everywhere, or to put down infernally caddish natives, today they came with order books for Schweppes.

Duckworth Drew, Drummond, and Hannay were all Great Britons; Bond's a Little Englander.

England, England.
James Bond is a meaningless fantasy cut-out unless he is tacked to the canvas of diminishing England. After the war, Sir Harold Nicolson wrote in his diary, he feared his way of life was coming to an end; he and his wife, Victoria Sackville-West, would have to walk and live a Woolworth life. Already,

in 1941, it was difficult to find sufficient gardeners to tend to Sissinghurst, and the Travellers' Club had become a battered caravanserai inhabited only by 'the scum of the lower London clubs.'

In 1945, Labour swept into office with the cry, 'We are the masters now.' Ten years later, in Fleming/Bond's time, the last and possibly the most docile of the British colonies, the indigenous lower middle and working-class, rebelled again, this time demanding not free medical care and pension schemes, already torn from the state by their elders, but a commanding voice in the arts and letters. Briefly, a new style in architecture. So we had Osborne, Amis, Sillitoe, and Wesker, among others.

The gentleman's England, where everyone knew his place in the natural order, the England John Buchan, Sir Harold Nicolson, Bobbety[1], Chips[2], and Boofy[3] had been educated to inherit – 'Good God,' Hannay says, 'what a damn taskmistress duty is!' – was indeed a war victim. Come Ian Fleming, there has been a metamorphosis. We are no longer dealing with gentlemen, but with a parody-gentleman.

Look at it this way. Sir Harold Nicolson collected books because he cherished them, Ian Fleming amassed first editions because, with Britain's place unsure and the pound wobbly, he grasped their market value. Similarly, if the Buchan's Own Annual cry of God, King, and Empire, was now risible, it was also, providing the packaging was sufficiently shrewd, very, very salable.

Sir Harold Nicolson was arrogantly anti-American, but after World War II a more exigent realism began to operate. Suddenly, an Englishman abroad had to mind his manners. Just as Fleming could not afford to be too overtly anti-Semitic, proffering a sanitized racism instead, so it wouldn't do for Bond to put down all things American. Ian Fleming

[1] The 5th Marquess of Salisbury
[2] Sir Henry Channon
[3] The Earl of Arran

was patronizing (Bond says of America, it's 'a civilized country. More or less.'), but whatever his inner convictions, there is an admixture of commercial forelock touching. Where once Englishmen bestrode the American lecture circuit with the insolence of Malcolm X, they now came as Sir Stepin Fetchits. The Bond novels were written for profit. Without the American market, there wouldn't be enough.

Little England's increasingly humiliating status has spawned a blinkered romanticism on the left and the right. On the left, this yielded CND (the touching assumption that it matters morally to the world whether or not England gives up the Bomb unilaterally) and anti-Americanism. On the right, there is the decidedly more expensive fantasy that this off-shore island can still confront the world as Great Britain. If the brutal facts, the familiar facts, are that England has been unable to adjust to its shrivelled island status, largely because of antiquated industry, economic mismanagement, a fusty civil service, and reactionary trade unions, then the comforting right-wing pot dream, a long time in the making, is that virtuous Albion is beset by disruptive communists within and foreign devils and conspirators without.

'(If you) get to the real boss,' John Buchan writes in *The Thirty-Nine Steps,* 'then the one you are brought up against is a little white-faced Jew in a bathchair with an eye like a rattlesnake.'

In Buchan's defence, his biographer, Janet Adam Smith, has observed that some of his best and richest friends were Jews. Yes, indeed. Describing a 1903 affair in Park Lane, Buchan wrote, 'A true millionaire's dinner – fresh strawberries in April, plovers' eggs, hooky noses and diamonds.' Elsewhere, Buchan went so far out on a limb as to write that it would be unfair to think of Johannesburg as 'Judasburg.' 'You will see more Jews in Montreal or Aberdeen, but not more than in Paris; and any smart London restaurant will show as large a Semitic proportion as a Johannesburg club.' Furthermore, like many another promising young anti-Semite, Buchan mellowed into an active supporter of Zionism, perhaps in the forelorn hope that hooky-nosed gourmets would quit Mayfair for the Negev.

Alas, they still abounded in London in Sir Henry Channon's time. On January 27, 1934, Chips wrote in his diary, 'I went for a walk with Hore-Belisha, the much advertised Minister of Transport. He is an oily man, half a Jew, an opportunist, with the Semitic flare for publicity.' Then, only two months later, on March 18, Chips golfed with Diana Cooper at Trent, Sir Philip Sassoon's Kent house. 'Trent is a dream house, perfect, luxurious, distinguished with the exotic taste to be expected in any Sassoon Schloss. But the servants are casual, indeed, almost rude; but this, too, often happens in a rich Jew's establishment.'

Sir Harold Nicolson's Jewish problem bit deeper. On June 18, 1945, he wrote in his diary, 'I do not think that anybody of any Party has any clear idea of how the election will run. The Labour people seem to think the Tories will come back . . . the Tories feel that the Forces will all vote for Labour, and that there may be a land-slide towards the left. They say the *Daily Mirror* is responsible for this, having pandered to the men in the ranks and given them a general distrust of authority. The Jewish capacity for destruction is really illimitable. Although I loathe anti-Semitism, I do dislike Jews.'

In a scrupulous, if embarrassed, footnote Nigel Nicolson, who edited his father's diaries, wrote, 'H.N. had the idea that the Board of the *Daily Mirror* was mainly composed of Jews.'

If Sir Harold Nicolson saw destructive Jews manipulating Churchill's defeat, then Ian Fleming, an even coarser spirit, sniffed plotters, either coloured or with Jewish blood, perpetually scheming at the undoing of the England he cherished. This, largely, is what James Bond is about.

Kingsley Amis, Bond's most reputable apologist, argues, in *The James Bond Dossier,* that in all the Bond canon '. . . there's no hint of anti-semitism, and no feeling about colour more intense than, for instance, Chinese Negroes make good sinister minor-villain material. (They do, too.)' Okay; let's take a look at the evidence.

The sketchy villain of the first Bond novel, *Casino Royale*, is one Le Chiffre, alias Herr Ziffer, first encountered as a displaced person, inmate of Dachau DP camp. Le Chiffre, a dangerous agent of the USSR, is described as probably a mixture of Mediterranean with Prussian or Polish strains and some Jewish blood. He is a flagellant with large sexual appetites. According to the Head of Station S of the British Secret Service, Le Chiffre's Jewish blood is signalled by small ears with large lobes, which is a new one on me.

The next villain Bond tackles, Mr. Big (*Live and Let Die*) is – says M, weighing his words – probably the most powerful Negro criminal in the world.

'I don't think,' says Bond, 'I've ever heard of great Negro criminals before.'

M replies that the Negro races are just beginning to throw up geniuses in all the professions, and so it's about time they turned up a great criminal. 'They've got plenty of brains. . . . And now Moscow's taught one of them the technique.'

The comedy soon thickens. In New York, Lieutenant Binswager of Homicide suggests to Bond that they pull in Mr. Big for tax evasion 'or parkin' in front of a hydrant or sumpn,' Here Captain Dexter of the FBI intervenes. 'D'you want a race riot? . . . If he wasn't sprung in half an hour by that black mouthpiece of his, those Voodoo drums would start beating from here to the Deep South. When they're full of that stuff we all know what happens. Remember '35 and '43? You'd have to call out the militia.'

To be on the safe side, Sir Hugo Drax, the arch-villain of *Moonraker,* is not a Jew. Instead he is cunningly endowed with all the characteristics the anti-Semite traditionally ascribes to a Jewish millionaire. He is without background, having emerged out of nowhere since the war. A bit loud-mouthed and ostentatious. Something of a card. People feel sorry for him, in spite of his gay life, although he's a multi-millionaire. He made his money on the metal market by cornering a very valuable ore called Columbite. Sir Hugo's broker and constant bridge companion is a man called Meyer. ('Nice chap. A Jew.') Sir Hugo made his fortune in the City by operating out of Tangier – free port, no taxes, no currency restrictions. He throws his money about. 'Best houses,' Bond says, 'best cars, best women. Boxes at the Opera, at Goodwood. Prize-winning Jersey herds.' Alas, he has also thrust his way into exclusive clubland, Blades specifically, where, in partnership with the nice Jew, Meyer, he cheats at bridge.

If Drax is not a Jew, he comes within an ear lobe of it. A bullying, boorish, loud-mouthed vulgarian, Bond decides on first meeting. *He has a powerful nose, he sweats, he's hairy,* but – but – 'he had allowed his whiskers to grow down to the level of the lobes of his ears,' and so, *pace* the Head of Station S, a chap couldn't tell for sure. In the end, Sir Hugo Drax is unmasked as ... Graf Hugo von der Drache, *Sturmer*-caricature-transmogrified-into-Nazi-ogre-turned-commie-agent.

In *Diamonds Are Forever* it is a smart Jewish girl who opens the door to 'The House of Diamonds,' a swindle shop. On the same page, we read,

> ... There was a click and the door opened a few inches and a voice with a thick foreign intonation expostulated volubly: 'Bud Mister Grunspan, why being so hard – Vee must all make a liffing, yes? I am tell you this vonderful stone gost me ten tousant pounts. Ten tousant! You ton't belieff me? But I svear it. On my vort of honour.' There was a negative pause and the voice made its final bid. 'Bedder still! I bet you fife pounts!'

Goldfinger begins to rework familiar ground. Goldfinger is clearly a Jewish name. Like Drax, he floats his gold round the world, manipulating the price, and naturally he cheats at cards. And golf.

'Nationality?' Bond asks Mr. Du Pont.

'You wouldn't believe it, but he's a Britisher. Domiciled in Nassau. You'd think he'd be a Jew from the name, but he doesn't look it. . . .'

Like Drax, Goldfinger has red hair, but, significantly, in the lengthy physical description on page 30 *there is no mention of his ear lobe size*. All the same, Bond, on his first meeting with Goldfinger, muses, 'What could his history be? Today he might be an Englishman. What had he been born? Not a Jew – though there might be Jewish blood in him. . . .'

Next we come to a real Jew, Sol Horowitz, one of the two hoods in *The Spy Who Loved Me*. Horowitz is described as skeletal, his skin grey, the lips thin and purplish like an unstitched wound, his teeth cheaply capped with steel. And the ears? This is ambiguous. Jewy possibly, but assimilated. 'The ears lay very flat and close to the bony, rather box-shaped head. . . .'

The Fleming Ear Syndrome reaches its climax with Blofeld. Blofeld, again not Jewish in spite of the name and easily the archetypal Fleming villain, has one hell of an ear problem. Blofeld, with old age encroaching, wishes to have a title, and so he applies to the British College of Arms, asking to be recognized as Monsieur le Comte Balthazar de Bleuville. Not so easy. According to Sable Basilisk, at the College of Arms, the Bleuvilles, through the centuries, have shared one odd characteristic. Basilisk tells Bond, 'Now, when I was scratching around the crypt of the chapel at Blonville, having a look at the old Bleuville tombs, my flashlight, moving over the stone faces, picked out a curious fact that I tucked away in my mind but that your question has brought to the surface. None of the Bleuvilles, as far as I could tell, and certainly not through a hundred and fifty years, had lobes to their ears.'

> 'Ah,' said Bond, running over in his mind the Identicast picture of Blofeld and the complete printed physiognometry of the man in Records. 'So he shouldn't by right have lobes to his ears. Or at any rate it would be a strong piece of evidence for his case if he hadn't?'
> 'That's right.'

'Well, he *has* got lobes,' said Bond annoyed. 'Rather pronounced lobes as a matter of fact. Where does that get us?'

Where does that get us? Jimmy, Jimmy, I thought, as I read this for the first time, use your loaf. Remember the Head of Station S, *Casino Royale,* Le Chiffre, LARGE LOBES, SMALL EARS. Blofeld has J——— blood!

Even more significant, Blofeld is head of an international conspiracy. Bond's most pernicious enemies head, or work for, hidden international conspiracies, usually SMERSH or SPECTRE.

SMERSH, first described in *Casino Royale,* is the conjunction of two Russian words: 'Smyert Shpionam,' meaning roughly: 'Death to Spies!' It was, in 1953, under the general direction of Beria, with headquarters in Leningrad and a substation in Moscow, and ranked above the MVD (formerly NKVD).

SPECTRE is The Special Executive for Counterintelligence, Terrorism, Revenge, and Extortion, a private enterprise for private profit, and its founder and chairman is Ernst Stavro Blofeld. SPECTRE's headquarters are in Paris, on the Boulevard Haussmann. Not the Avenue d'Iéna, the richest street in Paris, Fleming writes, because 'too many of the landlords and tenants in the Avenue d'Iéna have names ending in "escu," "ovitch," "ski," and "stein," and these are sometimes not the ending of respectable names.' If you stopped at SPECTRE's headquarters, at 136 *bis* Boul. Haussmann, you would find a discreetly glittering brass plate that says 'FIRCO' and, underneath, *Fraternité Internationale de la Résistance Contre l'Oppression.* FIRCO's stated aim is to keep alive the ideals that flourished during the last war among members of all resistance groups. It was most active during International Refugee Year.

Looked at another way, just as we have learned that Mr. Big may be forking out Moscow gold to pay for race riots in the United States, so a seemingly humanitarian refugee organization examined closely may be a front for an international conspiracy of evil-doers.

SMERSH and SPECTRE are both inclined to secret congresses, usually called to plot the political or financial ruin or even the physical destruction of the freedom-loving west. As secret organizations go, SMERSH is growth stuff. As described in *Casino Royale*, in 1953, it was 'believed to consist of only a few hundred operatives of very high quality,' but only two years later, as set out in *From Russia, With Love*, SMERSH employed a total of 40,000 men and women. Its headquarters had also moved from Leningrad to a rather posh set-up in Moscow, which I take to be a sign of favour. In *Goldfinger*, there is a SMERSH-inspired secret congress of America's leading mobsters brought together with the object of sacking Fort Knox. The initial covert meeting of SPECTRE, elaborately described in *Thunderball*, reveals a conspiracy to steal two atomic weapons from a NATO airplane and then threaten the British prime minister with the nuclear destruction of a major city unless a ransom of 100 million pounds sterling is forthcoming. SPECTRE next conspires against England in *On Her Majesty's Secret Service*. Blofeld, the organization's evil genius, has retired to a Swiss plateau and hypnotized some lovely British girls, infecting them with deadly crop and livestock diseases which they are to carry back to England, spreading pestilence.

Earlier, John Buchan, 1st Lord Tweedsmuir of Elsfield, Governor-General of Canada, and author of *The Thirty-Nine Steps* and four other Richard Hannay novels, was also obsessed with vile plots against Albion, but felt no need to equivocate. We are barely into *The Thirty-Nine Steps*, when we are introduced to Scudder, the brave and good spy, whom Hannay takes to be 'a sharp, restless fellow, who always wanted to get down to the roots of things.' Scudder tells Hannay that behind all the governments and the armies there was a big subterranean movement going on, engineered by a very dangerous people. Most of them were the sort of educated anarchists that make revolutions, but beside them there were financiers who were playing for money. It suited the books of both classes of conspirators to set Europe by the ears.

When I asked Why, he said that the anarchist lot thought it would give them their chance . . . they looked to see a new world emerge. The capitalists would . . . make fortunes by buying up the wreckage. Capital, he said, had no conscience and no fatherland. Besides, the Jew was behind it, and the Jew hated Russia worse than hell.

'Do you wonder?' he cried. 'For three hundred years they have been persecuted, and this is the return match for the *pogroms*. The Jew is everywhere, but you have to go far down the backstairs to find him. Take any big Teutonic business concern. If you have dealings with it the first man you meet is Prince *von und zu* Something, an elegant young man who talks Eton-and-Harrow English. But he cuts no ice. If your business is big, you get behind him and find a prognathous Westphalian with a retreating brow and the manners of a hog. . . . But if you're on the biggest kind of job and are bound to get to the real boss, ten to one you are brought up against a little white-faced Jew in a bathchair with an eye like a rattlesnake. Yes, sir, he is the man who is ruling the world just now, and he has his knife in the Empire of the Tzar, because his aunt was outraged and his father flogged in some one-horse location on the Volga.'

The clear progenitor of these conspiracies against England is the notorious anti-Semitic forgery, *The Protocols of the Elders of Zion,* which first appeared in western Europe in 1920 and had, by 1930, been circulated throughout the world in millions of copies. The *Protocols* were used to incite massacres of Jews during the Russian civil war. Earlier, they were especially helpful in fomenting the pogrom at Kishinev in Bessarabia in 1903. From Russia, the *Protocols* travelled to Nazi Germany. Recently, they were serialized in a Cairo newspaper.

The history of the *Protocols*, and just how they were tortuously evolved from another forgery, *Dialogue aux Enfers entre Montesquieu et Machiavel,* by a French lawyer called Maurice Joly, in 1864, has already been definitely traced by Norman Cohn in his *Warrant For Genocide*; and so I will limit myself to brief comments here.

Editions of the *Protocols* are often preceded by an earlier invention, *The Rabbi's Speech,* that could easily serve as a model for later dissertations on the glories of power and evil as revealed to Bond by Goldfinger, Drax, and Blofeld.

Like Auric Goldfinger, the Rabbi believes gold is the strength, the recompense, the sum of everything man fears and craves. 'The day,' he says, 'when we shall have made ourselves the sole possessors of all the gold in the world, the real power will be in our hands.' Like Sir Hugo Drax, the Rabbi understands the need for market manipulation. 'The surest means of attaining [power] is to have supreme control over all industrial, financial, and commercial operation....' SMERSH would envy the Rabbi's political acumen. 'So far as possible we must talk to the proletariat.... We will drive them to upheavals, to revolutions; and each of these catastrophes marks a big step forward for our ... sole aim – world domination.'

The twenty-four protocols purport to be made up of lectures delivered to the Jewish secret government, the Elders of Zion, on how to achieve world domination. Tangled and contradictory, the main idea is that the Jews, spreading confusion and terror, will eventually take over the globe. Like SPECTRE, they will use liberalism as a front. Like Mr. Big, they will foster discontent and unrest. The common people will be directed to overthrow their rulers and then a despot will be put in power. As there are more evil than good men in the world, force – the Elders have concluded – is the only sure means of government. Underground railways – a big feature in all versions of the *Protocols* – will be constructed in major cities, so that the Elders could counter any organized rebellion by blowing capital cities to smithereens – a recurring threat in the Bond novels (*Moonraker, Thunderball*).

In fact, the more one scrutinizes the serpentine plots in Ian Fleming's novels, the more it would seem that the Elders *are* in conspiracy against England. Not only are they threatening to blow up London, but they would seize the largest store of the world's gold, back disruptive labour disputes, run dope into the country ('Risico') and infect British crops and livestock with deadly pests.

In our time, no books, no films, have enjoyed such a dazzling international success as the James Bond stories, but the impact was not instantaneous. When *Casino Royale* appeared in 1953 the reviews were good, but three American publishers rejected the book and sales were mediocre, which was a sore disappointment to Bond's unabashedly self-promoting author, Ian Fleming, then forty-three years old.

By the spring of 1966 the thirteen Bond novels had been translated into twenty-six different languages and sold more than forty-five million copies. The movie versions of *Doctor No, From Russia With Love, Goldfinger*, and *Thunderball,* had been seen by some hundred million people and were in fact among the most profitable ever produced. Bond has spawned a flock of imitators, including Matt Helm, Quiller, and Boysie Oakes. More than two hundred commercial products, ranging from men's toiletries to bubble gum, have been authorised to carry the official Bond trademark. Only recently, after a fantastic run, has the boom in Bond begun to slump.

The success of Bond is all the more intriguing because Ian Fleming was such an appalling writer. He had no sense of place that scratched deeper than Sunday supplement travel articles or route maps, a much-favoured device. His celebrated use of insider's facts and O.K. brand names, especially about gunmanship and the international high life, has been faulted again and again. Eric Ambler and Graham Greene (in his entertainments) have written vastly superior spy stories and when Fleming ventured into the American underworld, he begged comparison with Mickey Spillane rather than such original stylists as Dashiel Hammett and Raymond Chandler. He had a resoundingly tin ear, as witness a Harlem black man talking, vintage 1954 (*Live And Let Die*).

> 'Yuh done look okay yoself, honeychile . . . an' dat's da troof. But Ah mus' spressify dat yuh stays close up tuh me and keeps yo eyes offn dat lowdown trash'n his hot pants. 'N Ah may say . . . dat ef Ah ketches yuh makin' up tah dat dope Ah'll jist nacherlly whup da hide offn yo sweet ass.'

Or, as an example of the recurring American gangster, Sol 'Horror' Horowitz (*The Spy Who Loved Me*).

> 'The lady's right. You didn't ought to have spilled that java, Sluggsy. But ya see, lady, that's why they call him Sluggsy, on account he's smart with the hardware.'

As Fleming was almost totally without the ability to create character through distinctive action or dialogue, he generally falls back on villains who are physically grotesque. So Mr. Big has 'a great football of a head, twice the normal size and very nearly round,' hairless, with no eyebrows and no eyelashes, the eyes bulging slightly and the irises golden round black pupils. Doctor No's head 'was elongated and tapered from a round, completely bald skull down to a sharp chin so that the impression was of a reversed raindrop – or rather oildrop, for the skin was a deep almost translucent yellow.'

Each Bond novel, except for *The Spy Who Loved Me*, follows an unswerving formula, though the sequence of steps is sometimes shuffled through the introduction of flashbacks.

1. Bond, bored by inactivity, is summoned by M and given a mission.
2. Bond and villain confront each other tentatively.

3. A sexy woman is introduced and seduced by Bond. If she is in cahoots with the villain, she will find Bond irresistible and come over to his side.

4. The villain captures Bond and punishes him (torture, usually), then reveals his diabolical scheme. 'As you will never get out of this alive...' or 'It is rare that I have the opportunity to talk to a man of your intelligence...'

5. Bond escapes, triumphs over villain, destroying his vile plot.

6. Bond and sexy woman are now allowed their long-delayed tryst.

This basic formula is usually tarted-up by two devices.

1. We, the unwashed, are granted a seemingly knowledgeable, insider's peek at a glamorous industry or institution. Say, diamond or gold smuggling; the Royal College of Arms, Blades, and other elegant clubs. This makes for long chapters of all but unbroken exposition, rather like fawning magazine articles. Sometimes, as with the description of Blades (*Moonraker*), the genuflection is unintentionally comic.

> It was a sparkling scene. There were perhaps fifty men in the room, the majority in dinner-jackets, all at ease with themselves and their surroundings, all stimulated by the peerless food and drink, all animated by a common interest – the prospect of high gambling, the grand slam, the ace pot, the key throw in a 64 game at backgammon. There might be cheats amongst them, men who beat their wives, men with perverse instincts, greedy men, cowardly men, lying men; but the elegance of the room invested each with a kind of aristocracy.

2. We are taken on a Fleming guided tour of an exotic locale. Las Vegas, Japan, West Indies. This also makes for lengthy, insufferably knowing expositionary exchanges, rather thinly disguised travel notes, as, for example, when Tiger Tanaka educates Bond to Japanese mores (*You Only Live Twice*).

Not surprisingly, considering Fleming's boyish frame of mind, competitive games figure prominently in the Bond mythology, as do chases in snob cars or along model railways. The deadly card game, Bond against the villain, is another repeated set piece. *Casino Royale, Moonraker, Goldfinger.*

A recurring character in the Bond adventures is the American Felix Leiter, once with the CIA, then with Pinkertons. Leiter, an impossibly stupid and hearty fellow, is cut from the same cloth as comic strip cold war heroes *Buzz Sawyer* and *Steve Canyon.* A born gee whiz, gung ho type.

If Fleming's sense of character was feeble and his powers of invention limited, the sadism and heated sex I was led to expect turned out to be tepid. But at least one torture scene is worth noting, if only because its connotations are so glaringly obvious. In *Casino Royale,* Le Chiffre pauses from beating the naked Bond with a carpet beater to say,

> 'My dear boy' Le Chiffre spoke like a father, 'the game of Red Indians is over, quite over. You have stumbled by mischance into a game for grown-ups and you have already found it a painful experience. You are not equipped, my dear boy, to play games with adults and it was very foolish of your nanny in London to have sent you out here with your spade and bucket. Very foolish indeed and most unfortunate for you.'

A roll-call of Bond's girls yields Vesper Lynd, Solitaire, Gala Brand, Tiffany Case, Honeychile Rider, Pussy Galore, Domino Vitali, Kissy Syzuki, Mary Goodnight. As the perfume brand type labels indicate, the girls are clockwork objects rather than people. The composite Bond girl, as Kingsley Amis has already noted, can be distinguished by her beautiful firm breasts, each, I might add, with its pointed stigma of desire. The Bond girls are healthy, outdoor types, but they are not all perfectly made. Take Honeychile Rider, for instance. *Café au lait* skin, ash blonde hair, naked on first meeting except for a broad leather belt round her waist with a hunting knife in a leather sheath, she suffers from a badly broken nose, smashed crooked like a boxer's. Then there's the question of Honeychile's behind, which was 'almost as firm and rounded as a boy's.' A description which brought Fleming a letter from Noel Coward. 'I was slightly shocked,' Coward wrote, 'by the lascivious announcement that Honeychile's bottom was like a boy's. I know we are all becoming progressively more broadminded nowadays but really, old chap, what *could* you have been thinking of?'

Descriptions of clad Bond girls tend to focus on undergarments. Jill Masterson, on first meeting in *Goldfinger*, was naked except for a black bra and briefs. Tatiana, in *From Russia With Love*, is discovered 'wearing nothing but the black ribbon round her neck and black silk stockings rolled above her knees.' Not that I object to a word of it. After all, sexy, unfailingly available girls are a legitimate and most enjoyable convention of thrillers and spy stories. If I find Fleming's politics distasteful, his occasional flirtation with ideas embarrassing, I am happy to say I am in accord with him in admiring firm, thrusting, beautiful breasts.

Unlike Harold Robbins, Ian Fleming does not actually linger overlong on sexual description. Or perversion. He is seldom as brutalized as Mickey Spillane in page after page. If anything, he's something of a prude. The closest he comes to obsenity is '—— you' in *Dr. No*. Mind you, this fastidiousness is followed hard by a detailed description of a black man punishing a girl by squeezing her Mount of Venus between his thumb and forefinger, until his knuckles go white with the pressure. 'She's Love Moun' be sore long after ma face done get healed.' Other, more exquisite tortures of women follow in further adventures, usually enforced when the girls are deliciously nude, but James Bond's language never degenerates beyond an uncharacteristic imprecation in *You Only Live Twice*. 'Freddie Uncle Charlie Katie,' he says, meaning fuck, I take it.

The Bond novels are not so much sexy as they are boyishly smutty. James Bond's aunt, for instance, lives 'in the quaintly named hamlet of Pett Bottom.' There's a girl called Kissy and another named Pussy. Not one of the Bond girls, however, lubricates as sexily as does Tracy's Lancia Flaminia Zagato Spyder, 'a low, white two-seater ... (with) a sexy boom from its twin exhausts.'

Ian Fleming was frightened of women. 'Some,' he wrote, 'respond to the whip, some to the kiss. . . .' A woman, he felt, should be an illusion; and he was deeply upset by their bodily functions. Once, in Capri, according to his biographer, John Pearson, Fleming disowned a girl he had liked the looks of after she retired for a few moments behind a rock. 'He had,' a former girl friend told Pearson, 'a remarkable phobia about bodily things. . . . I'm certain he would never have tied a cut finger for me. I feel he would also have preferred me not to eat and drink as well.' Fleming once told Barbara Griggs of the London *Evening Standard* 'that women simply are not clean – absolutely filthy, the whole lot of them. Englishwomen simply do not wash and scrub enough.' So, added to the image of James Bond, never travelling without an armoury of electronic devices, the latest in computerized death-dealing gadgetry, one now suspects his fastidious creator also lugged an old-fashioned douche bag with him everywhere.

Bond is well worth looking at in juxtaposition to his inventor, Ian Fleming.

In *Casino Royale,* Bond, staked by British Intelligence, plays a deadly game of baccarat at Royale-les-Eaux with Le Chiffre of SMERSH, and wins a phenomenal sum, thereby depriving the USSR of its budget for subversion in France. This adventure, Fleming was fond of saying, was based on a war-time trip to Lisbon with Admiral Godfrey of Naval Intelligence. At the casino, Fleming said, he engaged in a baccarat battle with a group of Nazis, hoping to strike a blow at the German economy. Alas, he lost.

Actually, John Pearson writes, 'It was a decidedly dismal

evening at the casino – only a handful of Portuguese were present, the stakes were low, the croupiers were bored.' Fleming whispered to the unimpressed Admiral, 'Just suppose those fellows were German agents – what a coup it would be if we cleaned them out entirely.'

Fleming, raised as he was on Buchan and Sapper, had other imaginative notions whilst serving with British Naval Intelligence during the war, among them the idea of sinking a great block of concrete with men inside it in the English Channel, just before the Dieppe raid, to keep watch on the harbour with periscopes. Or to freeze clouds, moor them along the coast of southern England, and use them as platforms for anti-aircraft guns.

Fleming's trip with Admiral Godfrey did not terminate in Lisbon, but carried on to New York. Armed, for the occasion, with a small command fighting knife and a fountain pen with a cyanide cartridge, as well as his Old Etonian tie, Fleming (and the Admiral) was supposed to slip into New York anonymously. 'But as they went ashore from the flying boat,' Pearson writes, 'press photographers began to crowd around them. Although they soon realized that it was the elegant, sweet-smelling figure of Madame Schiaperelli who was attracting the cameras, the damage was done. That evening the chief of British Naval Intelligence was to be seen in the background of all the press photographs of the famous French couturière arriving in New York.'

Fleming said he wrote his first novel, *Casino Royale*, at Goldeneye, his Jamaica home, in 1952, to 'take his mind off the shock of getting married at the age of forty-three.' It seems possible that the inspiration for his villain, Le Chiffre, was The Great Beast 666, necromancer Aleister Crowley, who, like Mussolini, had the whites of his eyes completely visible round the iris. Crowley, incidentally, was also the model for the first novel by Fleming's literary hero, Somerset Maugham.

M, also initially introduced in *Casino Royale*, was arguably a composite figure based on Admiral Godfrey and Sir Robert

Menzies, Eton and the Life Guards. M remains an obstinately unsympathetic figure even to Bond admirers. '... it may be obvious,' Amis writes, 'why M's frosty, damnably clear eyes are damnably clear. No thought is taking place behind them.' Whilst John Pearson writes of Bond's relationship with M, 'never has such cool ingratitude produced such utter loyalty.' If Bond's father-figure of a villain, Le Chiffre, threatens him with castration in his first adventure, then Bond, last time out (*The Man With The Golden Gun*) is discovered brainwashed in the opening pages and attempts to assassinate M. The unpermissive M. 'In particular,' Amis writes, 'M disapproves of Bond's "womanizing," though he never says so directly, and would evidently prefer him not to form a permanent attachment either. He barely conceals his glee at the news that Bond is after all not going to marry Tiffany Case. This is perhaps more the attitude of a doting mother than a father.'

A really perceptive observation, for Fleming, as a boy, was frightened of his stern and demanding mother and did in fact call her M.

Pearson writes in *The Life of Ian Fleming*:

Apart from Le Chiffre, M, and Vesper Lynd, the minor characters in *Casino Royale* are the merest shadows with names attached. The only other character who matters is Ian Fleming himself. For James Bond is not really a character in this book. He is a mouthpiece for the man who inhabits him, a dummy for him to hang his clothes on, a zombie to perform the dreams of violence and daring which fascinate his creator. It is only because Fleming holds so little of himself back, because he talks and dreams so freely through the device of James Bond, that the book has such readability. *Casino Royale* is really an experiment in the autobiography of dreams.

Without a doubt, Fleming's dream conception of himself was James Bond, gay adventurer, two-fisted soldier of fortune, and, in the Hannay tradition, ever the complete gentleman.

Bond renounces his occasionally vast gambling gains, donating his winnings to a service widows' fund; he is self-mocking about his heroics, avoids publicity, and once offered a knighthood, in *The Man With The Golden Gun,* he turns it down bashfully because, 'He has never been a public figure and did not wish to become one ... there was one thing above all he treasured. His privacy. His anonymity.'

Yet even as Hannay's creator, John Buchan, was a man of prodigious drive and ambition, so Ian Fleming was a chap with his eye always resolutely on the main chance.

'Most authors, particularly when they begin,' Pearson writes dryly, 'leave details of publication to their agents or to the goodwill of the publisher.' No so Fleming, who instantly submitted a plan for 'Advertising and Promotion' to Jonathan Cape. Copies of *Casino Royale* were ready by March 1953. Without delay, Fleming wrote a letter to the editors of all Lord Kemsley's provincial newspapers, sending it off with an autographed copy of his book. 'Dr. Jekyll has written this blatant thriller in his spare time, and it may amuse you. If you don't think it too puerile for Sheffield (or Stockport, Macclesfield, Middlesbrough, Blackburn, etc.) it would be wonderful if you would hand a copy with a pair of tongs to your reviewer.'

This jokey little note, properly read, was an order from the bridge to the chaps on the lower-deck, for Fleming was a known intimate of Lord Kemsley's as well as foreign news manager of the *Sunday Times,* then the Kemsley flagship, so to speak.

Fleming also astutely sent a copy of his novel to Somerset Maugham, who replied, 'It goes with a swing from the first page to the last and is really thrilling all through. ... You really managed to get the tension to the highest possible pitch.' If James Bond would have cherished such a private tribute from an old man, Ian Fleming immediately grasped its commercial potential, and wrote back, 'Dear Willie, I have just got your letter. When I am 79 shall I waste my time reading such a book and taking the trouble to write to the author in my own hand?

I pray so, but I doubt it. I am even more flattered and impressed after catching a glimpse of the empestered life you lead at Cap Ferrat, deluged with fan mail, besieged by the press, inundated with bumpf of one sort or another.... Is it bad literary manners to ask if my publishers may quote from your letter? Please advise me – as a "parain" not as a favour to me and my publishers.'

Maugham replied, 'Please don't use what I said about your book to advertise it.'

As the sales of *Casino Royale* were disappointing, Fleming turned to writing the influential Atticus gossip column in the *Sunday Times*, which provided him with a convenient platform to flatter those whose favours he sought. After Lord Kemsley refused to run a *Sunday Times* Portrait Gallery puff of Lord Beaverbrook on his seventy-sixth birthday, he did allow Fleming, following some special pleading, to celebrate Beaverbrook in his column. 'History will have to decide whether he or Northcliffe was the greatest newspaperman of this half century. In the sense that he combines rare journalistic flair, the rare quality of wonder . . . with courage and vitality . . . the verdict may quite possibly go to Lord Beaverbrook. . . .'

Beaverbrook, who had an insatiable appetite for flattery, bought the serial rights to the next Bond novel and later ran a Bond comic strip in the *Daily Express*.

Once Macmillans undertook to publish *Casiono Royale* in America, the Fleming self-advertisement campaign accelerated. Fleming wrote to a friend asking him to influence Walter Winchell into plugging the book. He wrote to Iva Patcevitch, saying, 'If you can possibly give it a shove in *Vogue* or elsewhere, Annie and I will allow you to play Canasta against us, which should be ample reward.' He also wrote to Fleur Cowles and Margaret Case. 'You will soon be fed up with this book as I have sent copies around to all our friends asking them to give it a hand in America, which is a very barefaced way to go on. . . . I know Harry Luce won't be bothered with it, or Clare, but if you could somehow prevail upon *Time* to give it a review you would be an angel.'

In 1955, the sales of his books still dragging, Fleming met Raymond Chandler at a dinner party. At the time, Chandler was an old and broken man, incoherent from drink. 'He was very nice to me,' Fleming wrote, 'and said he liked my first book, *Casino Royale,* but he didn't really want to talk about anything except the loss of his wife, about which he expressed himself with a nakedness that embarrassed me while endearing him to me.'

If the battered old writer, whom Fleming professed to admire, was tragically self-absorbed, he was, all the same, instantly sent a copy of Fleming's forthcoming *Live And Let Die.* 'A few days later,' Pearson writes, 'Chandler telephoned Fleming to say how much he had enjoyed it, and went on to ask the author – vaguely, perhaps – if he would care for him to endorse the book for the benefit of his publishers – the kind of thing he was always refusing to do in the United States and a subject on which in his published letters, he displays such ferocious cynicism. 'Rather unattractively,' Fleming wrote later, 'I took him up on his suggestion.'

Chandler was as good as his word, Pearson goes on to say, 'although it sounds as if it was rather a struggle. On May 25 he wrote pathetically to Fleming apologizing for taking so long – "in fact, lately I have had a very difficult time reading at all." ' But a week later he came through for Fleming, his blurb beginning, 'Ian Fleming is probably the most *forceful* and *driving* writer of what I suppose still must be called thrillers in England. . . .' (Emphasis mine.) Chandler's letter of praise ended, somewhat ambiguously, 'If this is any good to you, would you like me to have it engraved on a slab of gold?'

Fleming was also able to find uses for a burnt-out prime minister. In November 1956, twelve days after the Suez cease fire, it was announced that Prime Minister Anthony Eden was ill from the effects of severe overstrain. It became necessary to find a secluded spot where Eden could recuperate, and so Alan

Lennox-Boyd, then Secretary of State for Colonial Affairs and a friend of Ian Fleming, approached Fleming about Goldeneye, his home in Jamaica. Fleming, flattered by the choice, neglected to say there were only iron bedsteads at Goldeneye, there was no hot water in the shower and there was no bathroom, but there were bush rats in the roof. He did not advise Lennox-Boyd that Noel Coward's home nearby, or Sir William Stephenson's, would have been more commodious for an ailing man. He did not even say that the Prime Minister would be without a telephone at Goldeneye. 'The myth of Goldeneye was about to enter history,' John Pearson writes, 'It was too much to expect its creator to upset it.'

Sir Anthony and Lady Eden set off for Goldeneye and Fleming sat back in Kent to write to Macmillans. 'I hope that the Edens' visit to Goldeneye has done something to my American sales. Here there have been full-page spreads of the property, including Violet emptying ash trays and heaven knows what-all. It has really been a splendid week and greatly increased the value of the property until Annie started talking to reporters about barracuda, the hardness of the beds, and curried goat. Now some papers treat the place as if it was a hovel and others as if it was the millionaire home of some particularly disgusting millionaire tax dodger....' Two weeks later the bush rats caught up with Fleming. The London *Evening Standard* reported that Sir Anthony, troubled by rats during the night, had organized a hunt. Fleming, distressed, wrote to a friend, 'The greatly increased rental value was brought down sharply by a completely dreamed-up report to the effect that Goldeneye was over-run by rats and that the Edens and the detectives had spent the whole night chasing them....'

The Prime Minister's stay at Goldeneye brought Fleming to the attention of a public far wider than his books had so far managed for him. It was now, Pearson writes, that Fleming's public began to change. 'Up to then he had been "the Peter Cheyney of the carriage trade".... After Eden's visit ... many people were interested . . . (and) began to read him. After five long years the "best-seller stakes" had begun in earnest. . . . if Fleming with his flair for self-promotion had planned the whole thing himself it could hardly have been better done.'

Fleming continued to type out his dream-life at Goldeneye, visualising himself as gentlemanly James Bond, but the self-evident truth is he had infinitely more in common with his pushy, ill-bred foreign villains, and one is obliged to consider his sophisticated racialism as no less than a projection of his own coarse qualities.

Two final points.

It is possible to explain the initial success of the Bond novels in that they came at a time when Buchan's vicious anti-Semitism and Sapper's neo-fascist xenophobia were no longer acceptable; nevertheless a real need as well as a large audience for such reading matter still existed. It was Fleming's most brilliant stroke to present himself not as an old-fashioned, frothing wog-hater, but as an ostensibly civilized voice which offered sanitized racialism instead. The Bond novels not only satisfy Little Englanders who believe they have been undone by dastardly foreign plotters, but pander to their continuing notion of self-importance. So, when the Head of SMERSH, Colonel General Grubozaboychikov, known as 'G', summons a high level conference to announce that it has become necessary to inflict an act of terrorism aimed at the heart of the Intelligence apparatus of the west, it is (on the advice of General Vozdvishensky) the British Secret Service that he chooses.

> '. . . I think we all have to respect (England's) Intelligence Service,' General Vozdvishensky looked around the table. There were grudging nods from everyone present, including General G. '. . . Their Secret Service . . . agents are good. They pay them little money. . . . They are rarely

awarded a decoration until they retire. And yet these men and women continue to do this dangerous work. It is curious. It is perhaps the Public School and University tradition. The love of adventure. But it is odd they play this game so well, for they are not natural conspirators.'

Kingsley Amis argues, in *The Bond Dossier,* that 'To use foreigners as villains is a convention older than literature. It's not in itself a symptom of intolerance about foreigners. . . .'

Amis's approach is so good-natured, so ostensibly reasonable, that to protest no, no, is to seem an entirely humourless left-wing nag, a Hampstead harpie. I am not, God help me, suing for that boring office. I do not object to the use of foreigners *per se* as villains. I am even willing to waive moral objections to a writer in whose fictions no Englishman ever does wrong and only Jewy or black or yellow men fill the villain's role. However, even in novels whose primary purpose is to entertain, I am entitled to ask for a modicum of plausibility. And so, whilst I would grudgingly agree with Amis that there is nothing wrong in choosing foreigners for villains, I must add that it is – in the context of contemporary England – an inaccuracy. A most outrageous inaccuracy. After all, even on the narrow squalid level of Intelligence, the most sensational betrayals have come from men who, to quote General G of SMERSH, were so admirably suited to their work by dint of their Public School and University traditions. Guy Burgess, Donald Maclean, and Kim Philby. It should be added, hastily added, that these three men, contrary to the Fleming style, were not ogres and did not sell out for gold. Rightly or wrongly, they acted on political principle. Furthermore, their real value to the KGB (the final insult, this) was not their British information, but the American secrets they were a party to.

Kingsley Amis and I, the people he drinks with, the people I drink with, are neither anti-Semitic nor colour prejudiced, however divergent our politics. We circulate in a sheltered society. Not so my children, which brings me to my primary motive for writing this essay.

The minority man, as Norman Mailer has astutely pointed out, grows up with a double-image of himself, his own and society's. My boys are crazy about the James Bond movies, they identify with 007, as yet unaware that they have been cast as the villains of the dramas. As a boy I was brought up to revere John Buchan, then Lord Tweedsmuir, Governor-General of Canada. Before he came to speak at Junior Red Cross Prize Day, we were told that he stood for the ultimate British virtues. Fair play, clean living, gentlemanly conduct. We were not forewarned that he was also an ignorant, nasty-minded anti-Semite. I discovered this for myself, reading *The Thirty-Nine Steps*. As badly as I wanted to identify with Richard Hannay, two-fisted soldier of fortune, I couldn't without betraying myself. My grandfather, *pace* Buchan, went in fear of being flogged in some one-horse location on the Volga, which was why we were in Canada. However, I owe to Buchan the image of my grandfather as a little white-faced Jew with an eye like a rattlesnake. It is an image I briefly responded to, alas, if only because Hannay, so obviously on the side of the good, accepted it without question. This, possibly, is why I've grown up to loathe Buchan, Fleming, and their sort.

In his preface to *The Bond Dossier,* Amis writes 'quite apart from everything else, I'm a Fleming fan. Appreciation of an author ought to be *sine qua non* for writing at length about him.' Well, no. It is equally valid to examine an author's work in detail if you find his books morally repugnant and the writer himself an insufferably self-satisfied boor.

THE HOLOCAUST AND AFTER

The Germans are still an abomination to me. I do not mourn for Cologne, albeit decimated for no useful military purpose. I rejoice in the crash of each German Starfighter. No public event in recent years has thrilled me more than the hunting down of Adolf Eichmann. I am not touched by the Berlin Wall.

That much made clear, let me add that for some time now I've been reading published memoirs about life in the Warsaw ghetto, the *Paradies-ghetto* of Terezin in Czechoslovakia, Treblinka, and the Janowska camp near Lvov, Poland. After all these years, the record is still terrifying, enraging, and impossible to digest more than a small chunk at a time.

Take *Scroll of Agony*,[1] The Warsaw Diary of Chaim A. Kaplan, for instance. Here German soldiers roaming the streets looking for Jews to whip and torture, rounding up girls for obscene sport, and smashing babies' skulls against lamp posts, is soon made to seem like the good old days, the high-spirited prankish days, a phony war once the more scientific 'final solution' is set in motion in 1942; and the *Judenrat,* the sometimes notorious Jewish 'self-government' answerable to the Nazis, is com-

[1] London, Hamish Hamilton, Ltd. 1965.

pelled, to begin with, to deliver 6,000 Jews a day for resettlement in the East.

Adam Czerniakow, President of the Warsaw *Judenrat*, committed suicide by poison rather than sign the expulsion order. Unfortunately, another quickly rose to take his place. 'The expulsion is reaching its peak,' Kaplan wrote (optimistically, as it turned out) on July 29, 1942. 'It increases from day to day. The Nazis are satisfied with the work of the Jewish police. . . . This criminal force is the child of the criminal *Judenrat*. Like mother, like daughter. With their misdeeds they besmirch the name of Polish Jewry. . . .' Others, especially those heroic men and women who were later to rise in hopeless but magnificent rebellion, brought undying honour to the same people.

The intrepid and diligent Kaplan was not a natural writer; he was clumsy, without a reporter's ear for dialogue or a gift for the telling detail, but all this somehow enhances his diary. Where art might have been inadequate, even suspect, the diary of a bewildered, appalled man utterly convinces. The Warsaw ghetto, it seems, was always rife with wishful rumours. Mussolini has been murdered. Hitler has had a heart attack. Roosevelt is intervening for the sake of the Jews. Another rumour spoke of extermination camps, mass murder, gas chambers, but it was not generally believed.

Terezin was something else, a transit ghetto for the Jews of Moravia and Bohemia. More statistics. Of the more than 125,000 Jews who were squeezed into this garrison town with sufficient accommodation for 7,000, some 33,000 died from malnutrition and disease before they could even be transported to the extermination camps. 'While the Jews in Terezin,' Goebbels said, 'are sitting in the café, drinking coffee, eating cakes, and dancing, our soldiers have to bear all the burdens of a terrible war, its miseries and deprivations, to defend the motherland.'

Before the gas chambers were installed it was commonplace for the Jews in the Janowska camp, near Lvov, to be lined up and shot, to tumble into a mass grave they had dug for themselves. Then, once the tide of war had turned, the S.S. felt it prudent to dig up the graves and burn the evidence. Leon Wells, who was compelled to dig with one of the death brigades, writes, in *The Janowska Road*,[2] that one had to be very careful sinking a hook into one of these corpses, already in an advanced state of decay, because it might break in two. The corpses were stacked in pyramids of 2,000 and then burned. Stubborn bones were put through a pulverising machine. Then another squad, humourously called *die Goldsuchern von Alaska* by the Germans, sifted the ashes for gold.

I could go on and on, the catalogue of atrocities is endless and after all this time still unbelievable, but in retrospect there are other questions. There is, for instance, the question of the Good Germans. By 1966, only twenty years after the holocaust, we had already witnessed the astonishing emergence of the Good German. Those dashing generals, soon to come to your local Odeon screen, who plotted against Hitler in 1944, or were so besotted with culture as to spare Paris. And let's not forget the sporting *luftwaffe* pilots of the Battle of Britain, who always behave decently, and the chivalrous submarine captains who surfaced after each clean kill to search the sea for survivors. These men, portrayed on the screen by such as Marlon Brando, Kurt Jurgens, and Peter O'Toole, all have one remarkable quality in common: they were anti-Nazis. In fact, seen from today's disinterested vantage-point, such were the number and charm of anti-Nazis in the German armed forces that one wonders how Hitler came to power in the first place – survived – fought – and damn near won. All the same, I must agree that these fictional Germans *are* credible, while the many real ones who surely knew about the concentration camps and the few who made them work are not.

Even looking at the actual photographs of the Warsaw ghetto in *Struggle Death Memory*, I find it difficult to credit. Big assured German soldiers, each one holding a rifle ready, leading a group of starved ragged school children to a railway

[2] London, Jonathan Cape, Ltd. 1966.

car that will carry them to the death chambers. The children did not know where they were going. They sang songs.

Other photographs show German soldiers grinning as they torment bearded Jews. There are pictures of incredibly emaciated Jews, lying dead and frozen on the pavement. It is all so foreign. How much easier, drawing on our own sheltered experience, to identify with Eichmann's stalwart son telling the press, 'I'll stand by my father' than with these gruesome photographs of swollen-bellied wildeyed Jews. And while we're at it, why didn't they resist?

What is surprising is that so many did resist. By the time the Jews were transported to the extermination camps they were so broken in spirit and body, so obviously deserted and despised by the world outside (their international socialist brothers, the Pope, England, America) that death must have seemed a deliverance. Earlier, going back to the days before the war, it should be remembered that many of the most astute of German and Polish Jews clearly saw what was coming and left for Palestine, England or America, so that by the time the war and ghettoes had come, the Jews had already been shorn of many of their natural leaders. Other leaders, too many, as has already been noted by Chaim Kaplan and Hannah Arendt, behaved dishonourably. Still, there was resistance, but how pathetically easy it was to stop, and how amazed and encouraged the Nazis were that so few world leaders outside cared what they did with 'their' Jews.

If a Jew in the Warsaw ghetto was bold enough to strike back or even shoot down a German soldier, an early incident Kaplan notes in his diary, then the next morning one hundred innocents, including women and children, were rounded up, tortured, and shot. If a Jew managed to escape from a concentration camp, as two men did from Janowska, then the families they left behind and many more were murdered as a reprisal. But once it became clear that death was to be everybody's lot, there was resistance in Warsaw and elsewhere.

How very, very difficult it was too. The Jews, unlike say French or Italian partisans, could not fall back on a friendly populace. On the contrary. Minimal help was forthcoming by way of guns and ammunition from the Polish underground to the heroes of the Warsaw ghetto, and those others who escaped to form partisan bands in the forests had not only the Germans to contend with. Anti-Semitic Polish partisans hunted them down on one side and Ukrainian fascist partisans on the other.

Let no one ask why there wasn't more resistance. Let them ask instead, as Chaim Kaplan did in *Scroll of Agony*, on April 12, 1940, 'Is there any revenge in the world for the spilling of innocent blood? I doubt it. The abominations committed before our eyes cry out from the earth: "Avenge me!" But there is no jealous avenger. Why has a "day of vengeance and retribution" not yet come for the murderers? Do not answer me with idle talk – I won't listen to you. Give me a logical reply!'

Kaplan did not survive. He is presumed to have been exterminated in early 1943. Leon Wells, who did survive, writes that after the war the need for vengeance slowly died within him. 'How can one live despising the world?'

Eli Weisel, another survivor of the holocaust, the enormously talented author of *Night*, returned to Germany seventeen years after the holocaust and found, to his regret, that he was unable to sustain his hatred for the Germans. He wrote in *Commentary*, 'Yet today, even having been deserted by my hate during that fleeting visit to Germany, I cry out with all my heart against forgetting, against silence. Every Jew, somewhere in his being, should set apart a zone of hate – healthy, virile hate – for what the German personifies and for what persists in the German. To do otherwise would be a betrayal of the dead.'

Speaking for myself, I am a believer in obligatory voyages,

Gehenna being as necessary as the heavenly spheres, and so I've been to Germany as well as Jerusalem.

On my first day in Munich, in 1955, I went to meet a friend at the American Army Service Club, formerly Hitler's *Haus der Kunst*. Drifting into the lobby, I was confronted by a life-size cardboard hillbilly which held a poster announcing that Friday would be 'Grand Ole Op'ry Night.' Over the information desk, there was another announcement that I used in my novel, *St. Urbain's Horseman*. This one set out Saturday's diversions. Visiting GIs were assured that promptly at 1400 hours a bus would leave for nearby Dachau: 'BRING YOUR CAMERAS! VISIT THE CASTLE AND THE CREMATORIUM.'

I was in Germany again in 1963, this time to write a piece about the Royal Canadian Air Force base on the outskirts of Baden-Baden. Young, distinctly small-town Canadian school teachers attached to the air base breathlessly assured me the Germans were 'a simply fantastic people.' So modern, so clean. 'We have a lot to learn from them,' a science teacher told me. 'From their leisurely way of life.'

The next evening I went to the Social Center, mixing with teenagers at a dance. 'What have you seen in Europe?' I asked them.

'Venice.'

'A bullfight in Barcelona.'

'Dachau.'

Dachau. The boy was only fourteen. His parents, he said, had taken him to Dachau when he was twelve. To my astonishment, most of the other children had been there too.

'Do you know what Dachau is?' I asked.

'They used to punish people there.'

'Naw. Like it was extermination.'

'No, no. They just hung guys there. They never used the gas chambers.'

'Who told you that?' I asked.

'The Germans.'

I asked if they had found Dachau a chilling place.

'It's not used any more, but.'

'Yeah, it was only during the war. They used to torture guys there.'

'Why?'

'Um, there were too many prisoners so they had to kill some off.'

'The Jews were against Hitler so they had to exterminate them.'

'What else?' I asked.

'It was,' a boy said, 'an unusual place to visit.'

An unusual place to visit and one, properly packaged, that could also be commercially rewarding.

One would have imagined that after the gas chamber no further suffering could be inflicted on the six million Jews; it had come to a stop, but no, what we hadn't reckoned with was insult after death. If the holocaust has, on the one side, aroused the passions of some undoubtedly serious writers – say, Bruno Bettelheim, Hannah Arendt, and Elias Canetti, to name but a few – then it has also, on the other, led to what must be one of the most vile episodes in publishing and film-making: the discovery that genocide could be boffo.

Over the years, we have had a spate of ostensibly worthy but actually sensational, sexy films about the Hitler gang, an endless run of scatological articles about concentration camps in man magazines, and a flood of paperbacks about S.S. brothels. A more respectable but no less distasteful aspect of this traffic is the middle-brow documentary novel about the holocaust. Leon Uris, for instance, on the Warsaw ghetto. And, in 1964, another novel by a more elegant writer, this one about the rise of Nazi Germany and Paris during the occupation, *An Infinity of Mirrors* by Richard Condon.

As some of the best films – say, Fellini's *Il Vitelloni* – get to look like novels, so more and more best-sellers take on the characteristics of films. I don't mean that they are written with a film sale in mind, but that they are *already* films. The technique is the same. The day is not far off, for instance, when Leon Uris, put down by the critics once more, may complain, holding up his tape recorder for all to see, that the best part of his novel was left on the cutting-room floor. Meanwhile, we have Mr. Condon's spectacular – a documentary novel that reads like a newsreel with action-packed people scenes between.

An Infinity of Mirrors begins innocuously enough, seemingly a novel not so much to be reviewed as counter-researched. To begin with, Mr. Condon informs us that he spent three years writing and researching his novel, and then he lists, in the manner of screen credits, some forty-six source books that went into the making of it. Thoughtful conversation about Jewish history from, I suppose, *Basic Judaism* by Milton Steinberg, *What the Jews Believe* by Rabbi Philip S. Bernstein and others; concentration camp detail from *Human Behavior in the Concentration Camp* by Dr. Elie A. Cohen and elegant homes furnished by (Sacheverell) Sitwell through his *Great Houses of Europe*; Eichmann's small talk, probably courtesy of that well-known writer of 'additional dialogue', Hannah Arendt. There are no costume credits.

The early pages of the novel, set in Paris 1932, are heavy with documentary detail. In lieu of establishing shots, we are told (and I'm sure Mr. Condon is bang on) that 'The National Lottery had just been introduced; Malraux had won the Goncourt; Mauriac had entered the Academy; Chanel had just launched the first of the dressmaker perfumes. . . .' And a typical researched conversation runs:

'Have you seen the American tennis player, Mrs. Moody?'
'Helen Wills she is called.'
'Have you been?'
'No.'
(Skip nine lines.)
'There is a delightful exhibition of nudes at the Grand Palais.'

'We went to the Montparnasse show at the Salon de Tuileries last night. It was quite successful.'

An Infinity of Mirrors also has what film people call a strong story line as well as plenty of hotsy scenes. The basic plot would fit a western or a thriller, but in this case it just happens to be intercut with the holocaust. The story, briefly, is about Paule Bernheim, daughter of a French Jew, the greatest actor of his time. Paule marries a German staff officer, Veelee, tall, blond and handsome. They go off to live in pre-war Berlin where a sexually depraved S.S. officer, who secretly adores Jewesses, attempts to rape her, and then turns up again in war-time Paris, where Paule has fled with her son. In Paris the S.S. officer has the son (half-Jewish) picked up on the night of an S.S. *razzia*. The boy dies. Paule and Veelee avenge themselves by beating up the S.S. officer and having him put on a train bound for Dachau. Only then does Paule 'come to realize' that now she is a monster too.

Such a summary, however, does not do justice to the big scenes and audacities en route. Hitler himself, for instance, is brought into the story twice. Once to congratulate Veelee on his soldiermanship, but most memorably at a ball in Berlin where he 'wore evening dress, extremely well-tailored' and made straight for Paule to kiss her hand. 'My dear lady, may I have the pleasure of bidding you good evening.' Hitler, it seems, is also crazy for Jewesses, but Paule makes up for allowing the kiss by kicking 'that awful Goebbels woman' in the ankle. Goering and of course Eichmann also enter into the action, for the story is barely underway when the separation between real newsreel content and fictional characters is dropped – tangles – and results in a suspension of belief.

All the same, it's only fair to say that *An Infinity of Mirrors* is immensely readable, rich in romantic detail of the high life. What Mr. Condon has succeeded in doing is to make the rise of Hitler seem glamorous and sexy. There is even a comic sub-plot about secret agents in the best British film tradition. My chief complaint, then, is not that Mr. Condon has written a bad novel, it is that he has written an immoral one.

Since the appearance of *An Infinity of Mirrors*, and other middle-brow novels exploiting the holocaust, there has been another turn of the screw. The Six-Day War of 1967. A metamorphosis. The Jews, or at least the Israelis, now seen plainly as something like Nazi conquerors themselves.

In 1970, an issue of *Jews in Eastern Europe,* a periodical newsletter edited by Emanuel Litvinoff, was totally devoted to Soviet newspaper cartoons that equated Zionism with fascism and held that the former was no less than a 'serpent to swallow the world.' In a typical cartoon, this one reprinted in a Russian journal from the East German *Berliner Zeitung*, Dayan, sprawled over the desert, one hand grasping Gaza, the other embedded in Jerusalem, is encouraged by a bedraggled, bloodstained Hitler. 'You are a gifted pupil, Dayan!' When Israel is not represented by its one-eyed general, it is seen as a tubby, menacing soldier with a hooked nose. Obviously, the intention was to inflame the humanitarian conscience of the left and fill Jews with shame, but it didn't work for me at all. To come clean, I was flattered. To think, our heritage being what it is, that this fragile rib torn from the body of Arabia inspired terror filled me first of all with a very sweet charge and, only on reflection, with indignation that it should be so grossly misrepresented.

It was only on second thought, too, that I was exasperated by Horner's facile cartoon in the *New Statesman*, April 17, 1970, which showed an old and impecunious Egyptian bent over a stick and watching helplessly as the bombers approached, women and children huddling before their tents in the background. Who is the Jew, the caption asked. Well now, if these *are* the alternatives, I'd rather we had the bombers and they made do with the sticks this time out, if only because it offers some assurance that, should they be required, there would now be planes to spare to destroy the railway heads leading into the extermination camps.

Yes, the six million again.

I'm prepared to believe that gentiles, not to say evicted Arabs *with a case to answer,* are as bored with the six million as I am with black necessarily being beautiful, and that they would be grateful if a moratorium were called, but the fact is six million were murdered. They won't go away. Though, admittedly, some of the more dubious acts licensed in their memory stick in my gullet too. So long as they were alive there was no room in anybody's inn, but now that they are dead everybody has become an injustice-collector, claiming the inheritance. In 1960, in Montreal, I heard a fatuous suburban rabbi invoke the six million in a plea for funds to build a synagogue banquet hall. In Leeds, several years later, on assignment for the *Sunday Times,* I came across an editorial against inter-marriage, in the *Jewish Gazette,* which concluded, 'Hitler did his evil best to wipe out the Jewish people. It seems that if we don't look out we will finish the job for him,' as if marriage to a Yorkshire shiksa was comparable to a trip to the gas ovens.

More recently, James Baldwin invoked the six million. Writing in the *New York Review of Books,* he addressed an open letter to 'my sister, Miss Angela Davis' in which he noted, 'You looked exceedingly alone – as alone, say, as the Jewish housewife in the boxcar heading for Dachau. . . .'

The analogy, alas, was hysterical, infuriating, and wildly inexact on several counts. Therefore, it did Miss Davis, who may very well have been framed, a singular disservice. Jewish housewives, bound for Dachau, far from being alone, were crushed together in their hundreds into each airless boxcar, there to stand with their children, going for days without water, enduring their own excreta. There were no press photographers or militants at the station to cheer them off. Or *Newsweek* cover stories. Or the promise of a celebrated trial, with or without benefit of Soviet observers. Neither were there headlines round the world, as in the case of Miss Angela Davis, for the understandable reason that Jewish housewives for burning were commonplace. They were not known by name, only by number.

Numbers to be partially redeemed it seems. For the Israeli government (to its dishonour, alas) has, in the name of badly needed reparation money, put a unit value on the dead. What, I wonder, is the *prix fixe* for a boy drowned in shit and how much settles the bill for a baby boiled in the fat of its progenitors?

Something else.

Blessed with hindsight, putting everything in cool perspective, as it were, we have at last come to appreciate that if so many Jews shuffled to their death, maybe (psychologically speaking) there was a certain complicity, and nobody is to blame. Or, conversely, the Jews are to blame. The tricky Jews who, inexorably bent on suicide, took advantage of the Germans, selfishly using them as a means to their end. And the Germans, we now realize, were betrayed by Chamberlain, the Pope, Roosevelt and those hard-hearted politicians who, demanding the proverbial pound of flesh, would not clap hands for a conditional surrender in 1944. Which would have spared the German resistance, say one hundred aristocrats and generals. Now a cynic might interpose here that if this was the sum of German rebellion, however tardy, then it was considerably smaller than Jewish resistance in Warsaw, Bialystok, Grodno, Treblinka, Sobivor, and even Auschwitz. 'Authenticated documents and eye-witness accounts do exist,' Eli Weisel writes, 'relating the acts of war of those poor desperadoes; reading them, one does not know whether to rejoice with admiration or weep with rage. One wonders: but how did they do it, those starving youngsters, those hunted men, those battered women, how were they able to confront with weapons in hand, the Nazi Army.... We say: weapons in hand. But what weapons? They had hardly any. They had to pay in pure gold for a single revolver.'

Yes, yes, but it must be understood that for a German to resist in wartime was also to commit treason. Something that needn't have troubled the Jewish conscience.

Why, such is our largesse today, even the TV serial is beginning to look back on the situation in depth. 'Equally riveting, more universally hailed,' runs a recent *Sunday Times* Intelligent Viewer's Guide to the Week's Television.

> 'is *Manhunt* (ITV). Here, too, are unexpected attitudes to well-worn themes – the Abwehr sergeant seems a nice chap instead of the stock villain; the escaping RAF officer is hysterical and unreliable; the half-Jewish Resistance girl a bit of a whore.'

Well, why not? It's a fresh slant. Like doing Shakespeare as a skin show.

Now there is more than the Talmud on one side, and Leslie Fiedler's prescient jokes notwithstanding, *gefilte* fish on the other, to the Jewish heritage. There is also the holocaust: the holocaust which is at the very core of most serious Jewish writing since the war. It is what binds Malamud to Bellow, the one having made the moral gesture of *The Fixer* and the other continuing to write the novel of the survivor's reflections and self-justification. It is what connects both of them, through Isaac Bashevis Singer, who carries Warsaw, as it was, in his mind, to the documentary accounts of events, notably Raul Hilberg's *The Destruction of the European Jews,* and ultimately Eli Weisel, our witness. Weisel's personal account of survival at Buchenwald, *Night*, seems to me the one book about the holocaust that should be obligatory reading, yet his other books create problems for me. Possibly the trouble is that such is the exigent burden of Weisel's experience and our guilt, that he is, as writers go, singularly unfortunate. That is to say, to praise his style, his art, seems diminishing and grossly beside the point. In fact, when Weisel strays from his direct experience of the *shtetl,* the death camps and after, when he attempts to spin tales, an indulgence readily permitted to the rest of us, I find myself impatient. Unjustifiably, perhaps, but impatient just the same.

Recalling his defeated father, Herzog thinks:

'I suppose . . . that we heard this tale of the Herzogs ten times a year. Sometimes Mama told it, sometimes he. So we had a great schooling in grief. I still know those cries of the soul. They lie in the breast, and in the throat. The mouth wants to open wide and let them out. But all these are antiquities, yes, Jewish antiquities originating in the Bible, in a Biblical sense of personal experience and destiny. What happened during the War abolished Father Herzog's claim to exceptional suffering. We are on a more brutal standard now, a new terminal standard, indifferent to persons. Part of the program of destruction into which the human spirit has poured itself with energy, even with joy. These personal histories, old tales from old times, may not be worth remembering. I remember. I must. But who else – to whom can this matter? So many millions – multitudes – go down in terrible pain. And, at that, moral suffering is denied, these days. Personalities are good only for comic relief.'

MAKING IT

The literary progeny of a brilliant, influential, but astonishingly smug body of New York writers, what Norman Podhoretz calls 'the family,'[1] has taken to flagellating itself, squabbling over who is fit to inherit the coat of many colours, in a manner that strikes me as deplorably inbred. And coarse. To carve each other up in earlier, less highly-publicized days, the patriarchs at least created magazines (*Commentary, Partisan Review*), went to the artistic trouble of disguising each other in novels, and did in fact produce relevant and outward-looking social criticism as well as memoirs of some beauty. Today the noisiest of the children, parochial school kids, speak only each to each, castigating one another in *Esquire* (Baldwin on Mailer), or in acutely embarrassing collections of essays (Chicago-cousin Algren's *Notes From A Sea Diary*), or in bitchy estimates of the other talent in the nursery (Mailer's *Advertisements For Myself* and subsequent grab-bags).

Something has gone wrong, profoundly wrong, when a group of talented writers disdain their natural material, which I still take to be non-literary society, in order to flay each other in print.

[1] Norman Podhoretz, *Making It* (New York, Random House, 1967).

If, in the recent past, the emphasis was on literary performance, now the spotlight is on the performer. It's the personality, not the writing, that is offered for our admiration. The prime and most compulsively readable exponent of this so-called confessional stuff is of course Norman Mailer, who is increasingly known for nothing but being Mailer – not so much a writer as the embattled, problem-ridden personality we cheer on. *Our* Judy Garland.

Something of a country cousin myself, only an occasional visitor to New York, I have, over the years, absorbed a juicy bit or two simply by following the proliferating family squabbles in print. And so I'm well aware (as who isn't?) that the children don't play nicely together. Take James Baldwin, for instance. He has the *chutzpah* to call Norman Mailer a middle-class Jew. 'I hope I do not need to say no sneer is implied in the above description of Norman.' *But,* Mailer reveals, not middle-class enough for uppity Jackie Kennedy, who doesn't answer his letters and wouldn't have him to the White House like that nice Saul Bellow. Nelson Algren, on the other hand, caricatures Baldwin as the lisping, effeminate Giovanni Johnson, and describes Mailer as Norman Manlifellow, a man wearing a sandwich board advertising himself and lacking in courage. Not so, protests Mailer, revealing in a hitherto unpublished letter to Robert Silvers, editor of the *New York Review of Books,* that after seven other chickens were too scared to review Mary McCarthy's *The Group,* cocksure Norman obliged. After Hemingway, such is our *cojones*.

And now Norman Podhoretz, baring his own flick-knife, has – ill-advisedly, I think – joined in the rumble. In *Making It,* he stands up for Mailer, a writer whom he admires, but, on the evidence of this essay in autobiography, still an undigested influence. Podhoretz admits that Susy Sontag, the youngest member of the third generation, had an even more rapid rise to attention than he did, but then she had the same rich black hair as the young Mary McCarthy. What clinched family attention for Podhoretz, he writes, was a long and unfavourable review of Bellow's *The Adventures of Augie March*. Bellow didn't approve, and wrote a lengthy letter of recrimination to *Commentary*, sending copies to a dozen or more people. Furthermore, Podhoretz writes, Baldwin's *The Fire Next Time*, his famous piece on the Black Muslim movement, was originally commissioned by *Commentary* and sold to the *New Yorker* in an unethical deal made behind Podhoretz's back. And so, if Baldwin thinks Mailer is a middle-class Jew, well, well, he turns out to be nothing but a grasping Negro himself. Podhoretz told Baldwin that 'he had dared to commit such a dastardly act because he was a Negro, and had been counting on white-liberal guilt. . . .' This, alas, is unlikely to be the end. Even now I imagine Baldwin is writing a piece that will explain how Podhoretz attempted to jew him out of *The Fire Next Time*, trying to fob him off with six hundred bucks when the *New Yorker* was offering twelve thousand.

On and on it goes, the titillating trivia, the snitching, without dignity or relevance.

Making It, Mailer's outpourings, the broadsides by Algren and Baldwin, all belong to a *genre* with intolerable show biz characteristics. To begin with, there is the arrogant assumption that a big name on a book jacket, like a star's mere appearance in a film, is a sufficient enticement, and that intelligent readers outside New York, like filmgoers in the stix, can be gratified, even dazzled, simply to be allowed to bask in the reflected glitter. As Dean Martin, Sinatra, and their obnoxious camp followers tease us with puerile inside jokes about the Rat Pack, or Richard Burton and Elizabeth Taylor retail the details of their private lives, so Podhoretz, Mailer, and the rest would seem to believe us thrilled by a behind-the-scenes peek at New York literary society, its scandals, its fevers. Well, then, let me get this much straight. I have a continuing interest in the *works* of Trilling, Dwight Macdonald, Mailer, Fiedler, Baldwin, Podhoretz, and other family figures, but I've had more than enough of the grubby details of their careerist adventures and feuds. Put another way, my reverence for *Ulysses* does not extend to an interest in the prescription for James Joyce's spectacles or his laundry list. I, too, suffer small insults, ailments, and tradesman's bills. But I am unable to create anything as splendid as *Ulysses*. Ultimately, the family will be judged not by its self-advertised intrigues, quarrels, and jealousies, which are, after all, what it has in common with other closely-knit professional groups, whether they be dentists or lawyers, but for its signal failure, for all the racketing so far, to produce one individual work of art as enduring as *Ulysses*. As things stand, though Malamud, Mailer, Philip Roth, and Saul Bellow especially, have all done some first-rate work, the family is most celebrated for having produced a succession of inspired Raschis (editors, critics, and pedagogues) with a weakness for boring symposium (*PR, Commentary, Encounter*) and without, as yet, a Talmud to call their own. No Joyce. No Yeats.

Among the younger literary commentators, Norman Podhoretz has shown himself to be an undoubtedly astute editor and critic, but *Making It*, aside from the engaging early chapters, strikes me as a vulgar, badly-conceived book. It is Norman Podhoretz's contention that he suffered a dichotomy in his American education. Encouraged, on the one hand, to pursue success and worldly pleasures, he was taught, on the other, that success was the worst form of corruption. Ambition, he argues, 'seems to be replacing erotic lust as the prime dirty little secret of the well-educated American soul.' and then he goes on to say that at the age of thirty-five he recognised that he'd rather be rich than poor; he enormously enjoys money, power, and fame, which is only shocking in that it shocks Podhoretz. Nevertheless, out of this contradiction Podhoretz might have fashioned an essay or memoirs as fresh and startling as "My Negro Problem – And Ours," which he rightly takes to be his most original piece. Instead he has force-fed a fat and gossipy book onto a structure unable to sustain it.

I do not object to *Making It*, because, as Podhoretz argues in his introduction, it's a confessional work and 'to the extent that it deliberately exposes an order of feeling in myself, and by implication in others, it obviously constitutes a betrayal of a dirty little secret and thereby a violation of certain standards of tastefulness.' No, no. I object because the book, touching, deeply-felt, when it deals with the author's formative years, rapidly declines into gossip and trade talk once he begins to mix with 'important' people. *Making it* is choked with the sort of anecdotes about Podhoretz himself, other writers and editors, that I, as another writer, would find immensely entertaining if told over a shared bottle of whisky, but committed to print embarrasses by dint of its triviality. If, as we were once told, opinions aren't literature, neither is gossip criticism.

Let us take just two brief examples. The revelation that Bellow wrote a lengthy letter protesting Podhoretz's review of *Augie March* is amusing, juicy stuff, but it neither heightens nor diminishes my feelings about the novel, and I look to Podhoretz, a critic I respect, for illuminations and to Leonard Lyons, if you like, for keyhole tid-bits. Similarly, the dispute with Baldwin. Baldwin's essay on the Black Muslims and Podhoretz's reply are both important pieces, the kind of writing I value, but the behind-the-scenes quarrel between them doesn't interest me.

Again and again, I feel Podhoretz fails to recognize his proper material. He will go on and on, for instance, about the hazards of the trade: his ups and downs with the *New Yorker*, writers' blocks, and what *Show* magazine paid. But he can actually dismiss in a paragraph the fact that for ten weeks it was his army job to interview incoming recruits and decide what sort of work they should be doing if they survived basic training, which seems a deplorable waste of fresh material.

Making It can also be read as the story of a raw young provincial, in this case from Brooklyn, coming to the capital resolved to seek out the company of the famous, and acquire fame, fortune, and social position. Like the incomparable James Boswell riding into London in 1762. But, where Boswell differs from Podhoretz is not only in having a Dr.

Johnson, and a redeeming sense of humour about his own machinations, but also in that he was consumed with curiosity about ordinary people as well, the passing scene, so that *his* making it is filled with lavish detail about the times, public hangings, coffee house dialogues, the theatres, public houses, bordellos, and streets.

A closer analogy to *Making It*, perhaps, Alfred Kazin's *A Walker in the City* and *Starting Out in the Thirties,* which can be seen as one book, is also loaded with tender detail about ordinary people. Alas Podhoretz, typical of latter-day family figures, seems to have an eye only for his own ego, an eye turned inward to reveal that his motives for writing are mixed, his ambitions sometimes crippling, and that some days he behaves opportunistically and other days he hates going into the office at all, which is to say he is no better, no worse, than the rest of us writers, shoemakers, junior executives, social service workers, plumbers, and so forth. This isn't scandalous, as publisher and author both daringly suggest, and which I for one, would not have minded. But neither is it news.

HUCKLEBERRY FINKLESTONE

Leslie Fiedler is one of the most enjoyable of wreckers. His fiction is charged with malicious invention, his criticism sometimes dazzles, but both suffer from impatience, a tendency to rapid-fire recklessly. This is a pity, because it enables more orderly, less original observers to be condescending about him.

The truth is Fiedler has written some spitefully funny, as well as hard but perceptive, things, especially about the evolution of the American-Jewish novel. 'Certainly,' he wrote in *Waiting for the End*, a collection of critical essays, 'we live at a moment when, everywhere in the realm of prose, Jewish writers have discovered their Jewishness to be an eminently marketable commodity, their much vaunted alienation to be their passport to the heart of Gentile American culture.' Huck Finn 're-imagined' by Saul Bellow becomes Augie March or 're-invented' by J. D. Salinger is Holden Caulfield. Then only a couple of years ago, Fiedler wrote in *Poetry* magazine, mixing serious and commercial writers together for the sake of a joke, 'Wouk and Salinger, Bellow and Malamud, Philip Roth and Uris (are the) bandwagon which travels our streets, its calliope playing *Hatikvah*.'

Fair enough. But now, playing clownishly on his own jew's-harp, along comes Leslie Fiedler himself with his second novel, *Back to China*.[1] It doesn't exactly break new ground, as one might have hoped. Baro Finklestone, the fumbling protagonist, is a variant of that all too familiar fixture in contemporary Jewish-American fiction (*Letting Go, A New Life, Herzog*), the displaced professor out West – a brilliant but ultimately inept and comic Jew trying to instruct the doltish young WASPs in spiritual matters.

Finklestone is a second-hand person. He seems to spring from literary experience rather than from the recollected past. Fiftyish, petulant, a born wise-cracker, he is not so much a person as a compilation of recent fictional Jews. A lampoon. A *littérateur's* golem. Teaching at a university in the West, he resents nothing so much as the other Jews there. When troubled, whether with the Marines in China twenty years ago or at the university today, Finklestone eats enormous quantities of salami compulsively. All he can recall of his religious past are the first two words of Kaddish, *Yisgadal v'yiskadash*. And of his dry-breasted Protestant wife, he observes, 'He had married Susannah, after all, precisely because he had not wanted to marry his mother, as most of the boys with whom he had grown up had so helplessly, so comically done; he had not wanted to huddle amid the remnants of a dying, meaningless Jewish culture.... Yet he had always bristled, had he not, at any hint of antisemitic scorn on the part of his wife?'

My quarrel, then, is not that Finklestone isn't accurately observed – it's just that he's been observed so often. He holds tenure at a mythical western yeshiva where Herzog, Gabriel Wallach, and Seymour Levin are also correcting mid-term papers – the university in the corn fields having displaced first the garment district and then Hollywood as a background for Jewish fiction. Briefly, there's been a cultural change. Once Jewish boys were hit over the head with rocks: today they're pelted with fellowships.

[1] New York, Stein & Day Publishers, 1965.

Back to China shifts rather awkwardly to and fro between the wartime China of twenty years ago, where Finklestone served with the Marines, and the West of today. Some of the set pieces are nicely done, but the novel as a whole is static, only sporadically funny; rather too obviously thought-out, each character is seemingly selected to represent and discredit a fashionable cliché. In a fantasy China, Finklestone sits at the feet of Dr. Hiroshige, a Japanese war criminal. In the West, he seeks the real *goy*'s America on the reservation, eating peyote with Chief Too-Many-Buffalo-Hides. But Dr. Hiroshige is an imaginary Japanese and the Chief is an imaginary Indian. *Back to China* is not so much a dead novel as a living essay – a fictional application of an earlier Fiedler essay, 'Race – The Dream & the Nightmare,' wherein he dealt perceptively, freshly, with real and imagined racial myths and guilts.

There is another possibility. Maybe I have misunderstood Fiedler's intention and the novel is actually an elaborate literary joke – a parody of *Henderson, the Rain King,* a satire of Jewish university novels, and, in passing, a back of the hand for Malamud and even Hemingway.

In *The Sun Also Rises,* Jake Barnes was impotent. On the last page of *The Assistant,* Frankie Alpine has himself circumcised. But Baro Finklestone is capable of an even grander gesture. Hiroshima has left him feeling so guilt-ridden that he has Dr. Hiroshige punish him by performing a vasectomy on him.

If this be the penultimate step in the development of the American-Jewish novel, I dread to think of what comes next.

STARTING OUT IN THE THIRTIES

Today we suffer from no paucity of critics who avow, all joking aside, that life's become too violent, too damned incredible, for the novel to cope with. Experience, they say, has suddenly grown too big and unsafe for mere fictions. So now it is only the highly personal journalist, armoured with ego, charged with a third eye, say Norman Mailer, who is of sufficient size to document the age's insults. An acceptable conceit, I suppose, if you're the type who hangs Cartier-Bressons rather than paintings on your walls.

Today we endure – or are lucky to have, depending on what you stand up for – a superabundance of system-makers, perceptive knockers, and happy pall-bearers for the novel, but in Alfred Kazin we have always had something rare. Something solid. Here is a man whose work has always shone with a refreshingly old-fashioned enthusiasm for literature, a manner of yea-saying that does not, as in the case of lesser *afficionados*, embarrass. On the contrary. Kazin enlightens us. 'I am tired,' he wrote in *Contemporaries*, 'of reading for compassion instead of pleasure,' and I'm sure it's true. Others may dazzle us with their destructive wit or outrageous theories, but in a time of so many tricksy, modish assassins, Alfred Kazin, almost alone among critics *whom we can respect,* has the courage of an unashamed lust for books and the literary life. A resistance to wind changes, what's in and what's out, that he shares with his British counterpart, V. S. Pritchett.

Kazin's unfashionable passion, his risky humanity, is what makes *Starting Out in the Thirties*[1] such a likable book.

Living as I do in London, the first thing that struck me about Kazin's memoir is how it differs from British chronicles about the same period, say Philip Toynbee's memorable *Friends Apart* or Spender's *World Within Worlds.* Toynbee and Spender, both middle-class young men, came down from Oxford at a time when the intellectuals were taking up the working-class, making it their cause. The literary life, however, was their unquestioned heritage, unless they turned out to be really rebellious. Kazin, on the other hand, was of the working-class, he had no choice in the matter, and he was astonished, almost to the point of slapping his cheeks on his way through the boiling streets of Brooklyn, to be even allowed entry into the literary life.

Alfred Kazin emerged uneasily, guiltily, in an era when, as he writes, you still thought of typical writers as rebels from 'good' families. But times were changing. In Saul Bellow's *The Victim,* Albee, the WASP going under, complains to Leventhal, 'Last week I saw a book about Thoreau and Emerson by a man named Lipschitz.' And Kazin himself writes of the year 1934, '. . . the banked-up experience of the plebes, of Jews, Irishmen, Armenians, Italians, was coming into American books. The real excitement of the new period was in the explosion of personal liberation which such writers brought in from the slums, farms, and factories,' and goes on to list, with their proletarian backgrounds, Robert Cantwell, James T. Farrell, Edward Dahlberg, Daniel Fuchs, Henry Roth, Richard Wright, John Steinbeck, Nelson Algren, and Henry Miller.

On this level, the American literary Thirties resembles

[1] Boston, Little, Brown and Company, 1965.

nothing so strongly as the British cultural upheaval of the Fifties, when working-class fiction came into its own here. Unfortunately, a further affinity with the British Fifties is that so many literary reputations were inflated, because we agreed with what was being said and did not care sufficiently about how well it was being done.

In other areas, however, the New York literary life was, and remains, vastly different from the British one. In the opening pages of *Starting Out in the Thirties*, Kazin tells us how as a young man of nineteen he was so upset by a John Chamberlain review of a recent book on American youth that after reading it he charged right into the *Times* office to tell Chamberlain what he thought. Chamberlain, furthermore, talked out the rest of the afternoon with Kazin. Nobody, I daresay, would ever barge into the London *Times* office in response to a book review. It simply isn't done. It's bad form. It suggests seriousness, an immediate and deeply-felt response; and such seriousness is usually equated with bad taste here.

In England, very few good writers seem to take anything seriously, including themselves. Self-deprecation, sometimes marvellously well done, as in the late Julian MacLaren Ross's *Memoirs of the Forties*, is the rule. But is it enough? Isn't *anything* serious? Look at it this way. To have been a socialist in the American Thirties, like Alfred Kazin, was possibly to invite the blacklist or worse during the years of the McCarthy hysteria. Boorish, yes, but it also meant that somebody was worried, actually worried, by what you were thinking and writing. It mattered. Whereas to have been a socialist (or even a communist) in the Thirties in Britain was, in too many cases, to have taken just the right step up that rickety ladder leading to the House of Lords.

Kazin is splendid at evoking the excitement young men of his generation (and mine too, come to think of it) felt over Malraux's *Man's Fate*; the sacrifice Katov made, giving up his pellet of cyanide to two frightened boys who, like him, are waiting to be plunged live into a locomotive boiler. He is characteristically generous in reminding us of his 1936 response to Clifford Odets, such an unfashionable writer today. 'How I admired Odets! How grateful I was to Odets! Even his agit-prop play *Waiting For Lefty* bounded and sang. ... Listening to Stella Adler as Mrs. Berger in *Awake and Sing*, I thought that never in their lives would my mother and the other Brooklyn-Bronx mamas know that they were on stage and that the force of so much truth could be gay ... the actors of the Group Theatre had all the passion. I have never seen actors on stage and audience come together with such a happy shock. ...' Yes; I'm sure Kazin is right. But the question he doesn't ask is what, after all these years, I'm still burning to know. What happened? How did so many talented writers come to abandon or betray us? Henry Roth retreating in eloquent silence to his chicken farm, Saroyan lapsing into self-parody, Farrell repeating himself, Dos Passos going over to Goldwater, and Daniel Fuchs, among others, setting up shop in Hollywood.

In defence of the old Hollywood, the Hollywood of the big studios with writers' blocks, Fuchs once wrote in *Commentary*, 'I think it is a foolish scandal that we have the habit of deriding these men and their industry.... What they produced, roistering along in those sun-filled sparkling days, was a phenomenon, teeming with vitality and ardour. ... Generations to come, looking back over the years, are bound to find that the best, the most solid creative effort of our decades was spent in the movies, and it's time someone came clean and said so.'

Well, I doubt it. I also realize that I'm being impertinent. On a personal level, what Fuchs and others do with their talent is none of my business. But I was brought up on these writers, I believed in them, and I can't help feeling betrayed.

Unlike Alfred Kazin, I actually started out in the Thirties. I was born in 1931, so I was not, like Kazin, unlucky enough to be a young man in a society in which sixteen million people were unemployed. Neither did the war, when it came, horrify me. The war was the best damn time of our young lives. What it meant to us, in the Montreal ghetto, was the first time our fathers earned a living. It meant more food, fewer family quarrels. Our first sense of plenty.

It was after the war, at the university, that we discovered the writers of Kazin's generation, and they seemed to speak directly to us. We were politically-conscious students. We had nothing so urgent as Spain to excite us, but even in Montreal we read *PM* and the *Nation*, we signed the Stockholm Peace Appeal, protested against McCarthyism, and still later demonstrated for the Rosenbergs. We experienced the Thirties in its second coming, so to speak, when it seemed that most of the American writers who had educated and inspired us were in political trouble. Why, we even grieved for the Hollywood Ten. Reinstated in the Sixties to deliver unto us such abundance as there is in *The Sandpiper*.

How I admired Odets, Kazin writes, and how we admired him too, but those films filled with 'social content' that he and other Group Theatre figures went out to Hollywood to write, star in, or direct in the Forties; those treacly, brother-loving films, oozing with noble Negroes and funny, lovable Jews, are now reappearing week after week on British TV and they are embarrassing, unforgivably embarrassing.

What went wrong?

After finishing *Starting Out In The Thirties,* I would still like to know what happened to the heroes of my student days, but in fairness to Kazin I should add that he has not set out to explain the Thirties, but to tell us what it was like to be young and concerned then. The strongest sections of Kazin's memoir are not those which deal with his encounters with famous writers, perceptive as some of his comments are, but the quieter, more touching chapters that evoke his own troubled courtships, the Brooklyn streets, his family, private rather than public faces. That is to say, Kazin's memoir is of small account as resuscitated gossip, but shines instead with the real writerly virtues. Finally, *Starting Out In The Thirties* differs in quality from other recollections of the period, at least those I'm familiar with, in that it is not charged with *The God That Failed* sort of recriminations. Neither is it sullied by self-justification or hindsight. At its best, it is reminiscent of Kazin's earlier, more poignant memoir, *A Walker in the City*.

PORKY'S PLAINT

Circles completed.

Only twenty years ago, following Faulkner, Hemingway, Fitzgerald & Co., American Jewish writers, fearful of being branded exotics, their fictions confined to the parochial narrows, learned to lacquer their unmistakably Jewish characters with bacon fat in the earnest hope of floating them into the mainstream. Now John Updike, composing a comedy of American literary manners, *Bech: A Book*,[1] feels obliged to burnish his contemporary novelist with chicken-fat. After the take-over, following Bellow, Mailer, Roth & Co., a mere *goy* would no longer be archetypal.

'... He was, himself, a writer, this fortyish young man Henry Bech, with his thinning curly hair and melancholy Jewish nose, the author of one good book and three others, the good one having come first. By a kind of oversight, he had never married. His reputation had grown while his powers declined. As he felt himself sink, in his fiction, deeper and deeper into eclectic sexuality and bravura narcissism, as his search for plain truth carried

[1] London, André Deutsch Ltd., 1971.

him further and further into treacherous realms of fantasy and, lately, of silence, he was more and more thickly hounded by homage, by flat-footed exegetes, by arrogantly worshipful undergraduates who had hitchhiked a thousand miles to touch his hand, by querulous translators, by election to honorary societies, by invitations to lecture, to "speak," to "read," to participate in symposia trumped up by ambitious girlie magazines in shameless conjection with venerable universities. His very government, in airily unstamped envelopes from Washington, invited him to travel, as an ambassador of the arts, to the other half of the world, the hostile, mysterious half. Rather automatically, but with some faint hope of shaking himself loose from the burden of himself, he consented, and found himself floating, with a passport so stapled with visas it fluttered when pulled from his pocket, down into the dim airports of Communist countries.'

John Updike is, himself, the author of more than one good book; he is a superb stylist, easily one of the most fluent of contemporary American writers, and also among the most engaging. I am happy to say I don't know what Updike's politics are, which parties he attends, whether he signs petitions or demonstrates. So far as I know he is not a regular on television talk shows, has yet to star in his own film or top the bill at a love-in. In an era when writers are increasingly celebrated as their own most finely-honed work of art, Updike, refreshingly, continues to be known and judged for his things, rather than his personality. And his things tend to be very good indeed.

Like Joe Louis yesterday, Updike today reflects only credit on his people. Uncle John to some, uppity *goy* to others, he is, to my mind, a living testimony to the fact that there is more to the American Protestant ethos than Richard and Pat Nixon, the Rotary, Billy Graham and *The Power of Positive Thinking*. In a dark time, when the editorial offices of publishing houses and magazines in New York abound with sagacious Jews and militant blacks, the diffident wasps usually venturing no further than the mail room, Updike is the offay in the woodpile. He is a clear demonstration that the besieged, vilified *goy*, given equal opportunity, is fit for more than binding or delivering books. He can also write them.

We need more Gentile novelists, they should be encouraged, if only as an antidote to Gore Vidal, John Rechy, and Hubert Selby Jr. For it would be sad indeed if non-Christian readers, already sufficiently prejudiced against the majority, were left with the impression that 'among them' there was only homosexual love. Or that their writers, from Sinclair Lewis, through John O'Hara, to Terry Southern, had nothing nice to say about the white American *goy* who, after all, yielded to the world Ike Eisenhower, vinyl, the hero sandwich, Norman Rockwell, the deep-freeze, John Wayne, Red Skelton, baggies, and *The Reader's Digest,* among other things.

Hence *Couples,* not Updike's best novel, retains a certain sociological importance. It did copiously testify to the presence, even surfeit, of heterosexual hijinks among suburban *goyim*. Looked at another way, it lends credence to the theory that John O'Hara was not guilty of special pleading. *Couples* also boasted a hero uncommon in contemporary American fiction. After so many *schlemiels* (Herzog, Portnoy), it proffered Piet Hamena, a man who worked with his hands. A carpenter. Somebody who could drive a nail into wood without severing his thumb.

Among other good things, Updike, filling his *goysy* office, has also written a memorable account of Ted Williams's last ball game for the Boston Red Sox, the aforesaid Mr. Williams being the very apogee of a breed of vanishing heroes, the last great white baseball player, before pitching became synonymous with Sandy Kofax, a Jew with an arthritic arm, and hitting with Willy Mays and other black stars.

And now Updike, emboldened by his undeniable success in portraying wasp America, has revealed a hitherto unsuspected strain of *chutzpah*. Never a member of the Jewish literary establishment, what Norman Podhoretz calls 'the family,' he has ventured in *Bech: A Book*, to caricature one of their number. Following hard on another white Protestant poacher, William Styron who, in his last novel, *The Confessions of Nat Turner*, had the effrontery to take a black man for his protagonist, Updike has surfaced with what I can only call his Jew-gesture. As such, as a spoof – or a *jeu*, as Updike allows in a coy foreword – Bech is, as one would expect, graciously written, witty, and precisely observed.

> '(Bech's) own writing had sought to reach out from the ghetto of his heart toward the wider expanses across the Hudson; the artistic triumph of American Jewry lay, he thought, not in the novels of the fifties but in the movies of the thirties, those gargantuan, crass contraptions whereby Jewish brains projected Gentile stars upon a Gentile nation and out of their own immigrant joy gave a formless land dreams and even a kind of conscience. The reservoir of faith, in 1964, was just going dry; through depression and world convulsion the country had been sustained by the *arriviste* patriotism of Louis B. Mayer and the brothers Warner. To Bech, it was one of history's great love stories, the mutually profitable romance between Jewish Hollywood and bohunk America, conducted almost entirely in the dark, a tapping of fervent messages through the wall of the San Gabriel Range; and his favorite Jewish writer was the one who had turned his back on his three beautiful Brooklyn novels and went into the desert to write scripts for Doris Day....'

But, alas, *Bech*, more a string of loosely-connected stories than a novel, is episodic and curiously uneven in tone. Here comic, there solemn; Updike seemingly withdrawing with an impish grin whenever he draws too close to Bech's marrow. Even so, the book is charged with charm and pleasures, especially for others in the literary trade. We travel with Bech from a cultural tour of Russia and Rumania to Swinging London itself, wherein Bech is delivered into the hands of his publisher, one Jorgen Josiah Goldschmidt, a Danish Jew with 'the pendulous profile of a Florentine banker' and a habit of saying, 'Bless you' to everything.

Very good fun indeed is Bech unleashed to 'read' on a southern campus, a perplexed hirsute Jew up to his neck in ripe, gushing young southern belles. In the most touching scene in the book, Bech and his bitchy mistress, goaded by an obnoxious young student, submit to a pot session, Bech ending with his head adrift over the toilet bowl, retching miserably.

Two small errors. Nobody ever flew to London from America by Viscount, as Bech manages on page 136, and I toss this in not to cavil with Updike over a tiny point, but merely as this chapter was originally published in the *New Yorker*, and it fills me with glee to fault their much-vaunted sub-editing desk. Then, in the most amusing and otherwise apt bibliography tacked to the end of the book, there was one item that jarred.

'Gilman, Richard, "Bech, Gass, and Nabokov: The Territory Beyond Proust." Tamarack Review, XXXIII (Winter, 1963) 97-99.'

Tamarack, being *the* Canadian literary review, published in Toronto, would never have stooped to publish an American critic on an American writer, lest they be accused, in the present overheated Canadian climate, of having succumbed to cultural imperialism. Such a piece would only have been feasible if Bech – admittedly, a possibility – had a cousin in Montreal. Or a mistress in the Rockies.

ANSWERING THE ADS

There are some ads I was never sufficiently intrepid to answer. Take this, for instance, from the now-defunct *Justice Weekly* (Toronto), once the only Canadian magazine with an international following.

> 'C-5605, Los Angeles, Calif., U.S.A. – Sophisticated, fun-loving couple, late thirties, no racial barriers, interested in photography, rubber and leather, discipline, group activities, will answer all sincere letters. Photo in first letter a must.'

But for many years now I have been answering the sort of small ads that appear in the back pages of British and American detection, adventure, and scandal magazines. My obsession began when I was a teenager, small and thin for my age, pimply too. I speak here, I should point out, of the Forties, when our idea of hot stuff was Zola's *Nana*, which we considered outrageously explicit; anything by Thorne Smith; and, above all, Kathleen Windsor's *Forever Amber*. So there was nothing outlandish in sending off hopefully for SPICY books, THRILLING games and CUDDLE UP HONEY pin-ups ('An Open Sesame to a lot of Good Times').

Predictably, I endured disappointments. *The Pleasure Primer*, with stories by Ovid, Boccaccio, Rabelais and Balzac, was an expensive gyp. And it is clear today that only the most retarded teenager would thrill to OVER SEXTEEN ('Prudes Won't Think It Funny') or *Open At Your Own* RISQUE ('Lusty, Gusty, and Busty'). I also doubt if anyone but the most picayune would now send off two dollars, as I once did, for a batch of RED HOT TIME Stag Party Cards ('Wow! Here They Are! It Will Put You In A Positive Heaven of Delight With The Prettiest!'). Possibly, the most salacious of these cards read,

'OF ALL MY RELATIONS
. . . I Like Sex The Best'

It would be a mistake to assume that the bulk of small ads deals with sex. On the contrary. The largest number of small ads in detection and romance magazines have to do with the special skills that dropouts can learn by correspondence. They tantalize with the hope of Self-Improvement, *quick* RICHES, and SUCCESS! When I answered Leslie Patton's ad in the New York *Daily News* he wrote me,

'When I say the secret I'm ready to give you made me "rich," I know the term "rich" is relative and must be qualified. A Rockefeller or a Ford might call me "comfortably well off." A bus driver or country school teacher would look upon me as being rich as Croesus. I'll tell you this however – I live in a $50,000.00 home in one of the nicest suburbs of Chicago; I drive a big car; my last vacation was spent in Jamaica and the islands of the Caribbean.'

How did Mr. Patton do it?

'The reason I can live the way I do is primarily due to the secrets I have learned in buying gold and selling it to the United States mint. . . . *And the gold came from the attics and jewel boxes and dresser drawers of American homes collected by independent gold buyers.*'

Mr. Patton went on to say that when he was a door-to-door gold buyer he used to pay 17 dollars an ounce and sell for 35 dollars, and he recommended that I do the same, assuring me 'that any child can be taught to test a piece of scrap jewellery to see if it is gold,' *as long as he owns one of Patton's Gold Buyers Testing Kits*, cost 50 dollars. 'I'm not a fellow,' his letter continued, 'to put pressure on a man. You must make the decision, but don't lose any time.' Even while I was thinking it over, Mr. Patton wrote again to tell me that there had been a new development in the gold buying field and he wanted me to be one of the first to know about it. Only a fool, he insinuated, would hunt gold door-to-door – a smart operator would enlist the local church club or brownie group to round up all the junk jewellery in the neighbourhood. '. . . you can have hundreds of people gathering gold for you. After you have covered the churches, there are the Elks, the Moose, the Rotary – the list is almost endless.'

True, but there was still the question of 50 dollars for my seemingly indispensable Gold Buyer's Testing Kit. Well, I had underestimated Mr. Patton, for he wrote me a third letter. Fifty bucks, he suggested, was quite a nut, but he was so determined to get me started that he offered me a special deal. Instead of cash I could send 'anything: rings, watches, chains, lockets, bridgework, crowns, eye glass frames, cuff links, fountain pen points – anything at all you can think of that might contain gold.' Mr. Patton also warned me that as I didn't own a Testing Kit yet, I was bound to be mistaken about some of the stuff I sent off, it would be plated and worthless, so he would test the stuff himself for me, give me an honest appraisal, and credit my gold against the price of a kit. There remained only one problem. 'I'm going to be leaving town soon on a business trip,' Mr. Patton wrote in a printed, undated letter, 'so if you want to take advantage of this offer, you'll have to send your old jewellery in right away so I can give it my personal attention. After I've left it will be too late as no one else in the office is authorized to pay

35 dollars an ounce for gold. So let me hear from you right away.'

Obviously, many people do respond immediately, for Mr. Patton can afford to run full-page ads in newspapers as expensive as the New York *Daily News*.

Contemporary fiction spills over with examples of the sort of man, meaninglessly employed, a drifter for years, who puts his last hope into answering a small ad. When Ginger Coffey, the Irish immigrant hero of Brian Moore's *The Luck of Ginger Coffey,* comes to Montreal he stops first at the YMCA, and there is immediately confronted with the butt-end of a man who is learning Personality Mastery by correspondence. In Evan S. Connell Jr.'s *The Diary of a Rapist*, which deals with the fantasy life of impecunious clerks in the California State Employment Bureau, Earl Summerfield, who is keeping the diary, writes of another clerk, Magnus, '... living with his sister and brother-in-law, one little room, a cheap radio for company. Last week telling me about an Arkansas farmer who plowed up a diamond weighing almost two carats. Asked if he was going to start plowing up his back yard. He didn't laugh. Serious and humble as a cur he says his brother-in-law wouldn't allow it. Now he's convinced he knows where to find one of the jewelled Easter eggs that belonged to the Czar! Heard about some antique shop in the suburbs where somebody noticed this thing on sale for five dollars.' Another case in point is *In Cold Blood,* wherein Truman Capote tells us that Perry Smith, one of the Clutter family killers, carried a treasure map with him to Mexico, a map that showed where Spanish galleons, laden with gold coins, had sunk. You usually acquire such a map only by answering a small ad in a detective or man's action magazine.

One of the most frequent species of ads in action magazines has considerable appeal; it offers not only a new career, but status, adventure, and a gun. I speak here of the private eye schools, such as Crime Research Publishers, Los Angeles, who wrote me, once I had responded to their ad, saying, 'YOUR

NAME HAS BEEN SELECTED. You have been selected to receive the Crime Research Course at (50%) Fifty per cent discount. To take advantage of this wonderful offer you have to act *at once*.' Among the eighteen lessons (cost, 23 dollars) there was one on Tracing, another on Shadowing, and a third on Observation & Memory. Enclosed with the offer there was a detective's badge, made of paper, it's true, but promised for graduation day was an OFFICIAL wallet-sized card that would 'serve as an introduction to all peace officers.'

A rival school in Chicago, the Institute of Applied Science, sent me a more imposing package, including the hardbound *Blue Book of Crime*, some investigation reports, a free copy of the monthly *Fingerprint and Identification* magazine, several brochures, and a personal letter which began, 'There is Money in Fingerprints! Be Sure of Your Share,' and went on from there to point out that, in the school's opinion, 'the day is coming when it will be required that every one is fingerprinted. Where will all the experts come from to handle this amount of work?' Where, indeed? Why, for a mere 145 dollars the Institute, established in 1916, with graduates working in more than eight hundred different identification bureaus in America, would make sure I got on board the fingerprint gravy train before it was too late. Of course proper training was crucial. T. Dickenson Cooke, Director of the Institute, who signed his letter, 'Yours for a better job' wrote, 'All the great men you can recall to mind: Washington, Lincoln, Edison, Tesla, Marconi, MacArthur – have one particular quality in common, and it is training.' In a later, more persuasive letter he assured me, 'I know hundreds of people all over the country, BIG people. I'll do everything in my power to help you make more money than ever before.'

In the Institute of Applied Science's brochure YOUR CHANCE FOR SUCCESS! THRILLS! A STEADY INCOME! the detective in the illustration wears a top hat, tails, an orchid in his lapel, and white gloves. In another brochure, drawings with captions illustrate WHERE WE FIND THE

MODERN INVESTIGATOR. A dashing chap stands at the ship's rail and underneath we read, 'Often the chase leads to foreign shores – voyaging is one of the irresistible lures of the fascinating profession.' In the next drawing the same intrepid crime buster sits in a theatre, pencil and notebook in hand. 'Little did the audience realize that in their very midst an international plot was being formed – and being discovered.' In yet another drawing our operator appears to have fallen on hard times. The caption reads, 'Little attention was paid to the poorly clad beggar sprawled on the next bench. . . . thru this oversight the bomb plotters were rounded up that very night.'

Does anybody sign up for these correspondence courses? In an interview with *London Life* magazine, John Walsh, who runs one of the largest private detective agencies in England, said that he has had several applicants for jobs who produced postal tuition certificates as a qualification. 'The tragedy of it was,' he said, 'that you got quite a few coloured people going in for it. Quite decent chaps, really, but they weren't detectives.'

Immigrants are most susceptible to Improve Your English courses, such as the one offered by Don Bolander, director of the Career Institute in Chicago, who mailed me a copy of his inspirational booklet, HOW GOOD ENGLISH CHANGED MY LIFE.

> 'ROY,' SAID THE BOSS,
> 'you've made yourself over in the last few months! You've picked your head up off your chest and developed confidence and determination you never had before. But what I like most is the way you speak and write! I've never seen so much improvement in a man in so short a time! We think you're ready for a promotion. Starting Monday, you'll report to the manager of your department as his assistant – and there will be a raise for you in your next pay cheque! Congratulations!'

I have also been in touch with the Creative Prayer Institute in California ('. . . deals directly with universal mind. . . .'), which was willing to pray for me for a period of two weeks to six months as soon as I filled out my prayer treatment card. Then the Broadway Institute of Drama and Elocution Inc. sent me a letter saying, 'There's A NEW STAR on the horizon ... YOU!

'LISTEN! The entertainment industry today is a multi-million dollar industry. Its success depends entirely upon talent. ... YOU may be the unknown star they are looking for ... the new face to thrill the multitude of our entertainment starved public.'

Writing schools, of course, proliferate in both England and the U.S. *'Think* SUCCESS,' the British Bennett College advised me. 'Let me be your father,' James Bennett, the man who made half-a-million dreams come true, wrote me. However, a quick flip through a synopsis of the Bennett College's novel writing course was not reassuring.

'Tricks, Tools, and Traps – particularly Traps – the worst trap, libel – what a beginner must avoid at all cost – how I was caught, and why – another trap, plagiarism – caught again, just trying to do someone a good turn –'

The TV Scriptwriters School, London, was more promising. 'Every television company is waiting with open cheque-books for scripts that come up to their standards. What are these standards and how are they attained?'

How? By writing to Creative Features, Potomac P.O. Box 2121, Alexandria, Virginia, which is exactly what I did. A week later I heard from Charles Kapitzky, General Manager.

'Dear WRITER,
CONGRATULATIONS! You've made a wise choice in your decision to purchase THE PLOTTER. We feel that THE PLOTTER has been called "The Freelancer's Cornucopia" for good reason! We hope you think so, too!
As you're browsing through your edition ... be sure to notice the BARGAIN RATES for a year's subscription.

'... Just think, for only $20.00 (ON EASY TERMS, OF COURSE) you will receive ... EACH MONTH FOR 12 MONTHS A BRAND NEW EDITION OF THE PLOTTER! ...
A bargain? Yes, we think so, too! And that's not all. ... you will also receive a FREE GIFT of a smart looking ROCKET ANGLE BALL POINT PEN when you subscribe.'

The Plotter (Sept. 1960) begins with some sound advice. 'First of all,' Kapitzky writes, 'study THE PLOTTER plots carefully. Determine which type of story you are going to try first – Action, Mystery, Love, Western, or a combination of these.' Then there are some general rules to follow. Start your story in high gear, and come the FIFTH SCENE it's time to 'Shovel trouble at your Main Character.' By the NINTH SCENE the writer ought to 'Pull out all the stops!' and by the tenth Kapitzky strongly recommends that 'by HIS OWN SKILL, the Main Character extricates himself from the Villain's trap. ... AND MAKE THE READER JUMP IN AND FIGHT ALONGSIDE HIM!'

There's more to the magazine than plots and instruction. Kapitzky's Writer's Mail Mart, for instance, is 'open 24 hours a day.' You can buy a Character Chart for fifty cents and, available at the same price, there is 'Analysis & Plot – The Religious (Prot.) Story.' I would also like to draw your attention to the Timely Article Tips Calendar for December.

'DECEMBER
1st.   The last spike of the Southern Pacific Railroad was driven today in 1881.
6th.   The first U.S. Naval Observatory was established today in 1830.
7th.   Pearl Harbor was attacked today in 1941.
14th. George Washington died today at Mount Vernon in 1799.

15th. The first edition of THE PLOTTER was published in 1959.

More good news. The Plot Doctor, François de la Roché, is always available to treat your literary ills. For five dollars, he will service a manuscript of 5,000 words or less.

The joke-writing profession is something else again. Its more modest practitioners, many of whom advertise in *Variety* or the insipid, poorly written British equivalent, *Stage,* offer original material for as little as ten shillings. Take this, for instance, from SMITH'S SCRIPTS, A TASTY PACKET. 'I got thrown out of a big store the other day. I only asked for some assorted tarts. Trouble was I went up to the wrong counter.'

My first venture in joke-buying was with a man who signs his letters, 'Your Fun-Maker, Fred Fortune.' and who sent me his *Original* GIANT FOLIO for a pound. Included in the grab-bag of mimeographed sheets was some Original Quick Cross-Talk for Straight (A) & Comedian (B).

A. Do you travel much?
B. I used to, but I turned it up.
A. Why?
B. I travelled in ladies' underwear for a year and caught cold.
A. I mean travel abroad – Norway?
B. No, I went the other way – To Italy.
A. Touch Florence?
B. I didn't have a chance, her mother was always with her.

For a further pound Mr. Fortune offered 'THE VICAR AND THE CURATE, Clean funny gags & patter for Comedy Clerics' and 'A SEAT IN THE PARK, Smashing crosstalk for Lady & Pick-Up Percy.' Two burlesque songs also available from Mr. Fortune were *If The Bed Breaks In The Middle Meet Me In The Spring* and *She Was Only The Sergeant's*

Daughter But She Wouldn't Let The Police Inspector. His FUN FOLIO was not without social content.

A. Don't you know the Queen's English?
B. I know the Queen's not French.
A. Haven't you had any education?
B. A college education.
A. Have you been to Eton?
B. I've been to Eton, Drinking, and Smoking.

Fred Fortune's mimeographed letter (THE ROAD THAT LEADS TO FORTUNE) warned, '*I* am the *Originator* of this particular service; others copy my Style but they'll never imitate the QUALITY.' Even so, I did write to Keith Cooper of Manchester, who informed me that, at the moment, he had 73 joke sheets for sale and the price was five shillings for ten. Among the items offered was 'a straight monologue entitled THE STONE... showing the way in which some people view RELIGION. This monologue will give offence to no-one whether they be Church of England, Methodist, or Roman Catholic.'

A well-known Hollywood comedy writer, Reuben Ship, told me that the definitive gag-file was compiled in the thirties by an empirical writer named David Freedman. It was born of necessity, that is to say, radio. Freedman, like many others, used to write sketches for Broadway shows and revues, routines that could run and bring in royalties for a year or two, when he was suddenly confronted with radio, a national audience, and the weekly need for new if not exactly fresh comedy. Freedman set his entire family to work, clipping newspapers and magazines in many languages, and compiled an enormous joke hoard with a scientific system of cross filing. Based on this HUMOR-HEAP or FORT KNOX OF FUN, he wrote or administered the jokes for the Eddy Cantor Show, the Rudy Valee Show, and others. Many of today's most successful TV comedy writers were once apprentices in the Freedman factory, though the importance of the two-liner has diminished considerably since the situation comedy came into fashion.

David Freedman's library of humour was, they say, ultimately worth a fortune, but other American material comes cheaper, as I discovered when I answered Billy Glason's ad in *Variety* and sent him three dollars for a sample copy of the PROFESSIONAL monthly comedy service, THE COMEDIAN.

'Dear Friend,' Glason wrote, 'WE SERVICE THE STARS – the biggest names in Show Business; COMEDIANS, WRITERS, HOME TALENT PRODUCERS, AFTER DINNER SPEAKERS, TEACHERS, PROFESSORS . . . COLUMNISTS . . . LIBRARIES . . . UNIVERSITIES . . . PENAL INSTITUTIONS, RELIGIOUS ORGANIZATIONS SUCH AS CHURCHES . . . and anyone else who has to use a bit of humour in their work. . . .'

Glason, who claims to supply 'the mostest material at the lowest prices,' offers the following material from stock. 'HUMORDOR FOR EMCEES, A Complete Encyclopedia of Comedy Material,' $100; 'THE BLUE BOOK (STRICTLY FOR STAGS),' $75; 'GIANT ENCYCLOPEDIA OF CLASSIFIED GAGS,' twenty volumes for $1,000; and the 'PEDRO COLLECTION, GAGS & ROUTINES WITH A SPANEESH FLAVOUR!' $25. Fun-Master song parodies, five bucks each, included 'JUNE IS BUSTIN' OUT ALL OVER, 2 versions, one A PREGNANT VERSION and the other a DIET VERSION . . . one is CLEAN, the other is NOT'; 'THE LAST TIME I SAW PARIS (MORRIS), 4 different versions, 3 rather sophisticated, the other is CLEAN'; 'WHAT A DIFFERENCE A DAY (DAME) MADE, good and zingy, if that's what you want'; and 'IRELAND MUST BE HEAVEN (THEY CALLED IT IRELAND) . . . CLEAN! An Irishman throws bricks at a Jewish friend who saved them and built a hotel.'

FUN-MASTER, Glason wrote, IS PROFESSIONAL. FUN-MASTER IS JEST-PROPULSION. He also warned that he made NO CHANGES, accepted NO RETURNS, and gave NO SAMPLES. EVERYTHING is PREPAID. Glason's FUN-MASTER MONTHLY, the mimeographed COMEDIAN, contained, as promised, AUDIENCE LINES, AFTER THE ACT LINES, BANK AND WORK LINES, CROSSOVERS, FLORIDA GAGS, HECKLERS, INSULTS, JUNE BRIDES, KNOCK KNOCKS, LAS VEGAS GAGS, ONE LINERS, RESORT GAGS, SQUELCHES, SARCASM, TEXAS GAGS, TOMMY MANVILLE GAGS, and THOUGHTS OF THE DAY.

Following, a representative selection.

STORIES: A space ship landed in the Congo and a Martian stepped out and asked a Congo soldier to take him to his leader. The soldier said, 'Lumumba or Kasavubu?' and the Martian said, 'Take me to your leader, we'll dance later.' ONE LINER: This year I'm going to vote a straight ticket, just as soon as I find out which party is going straight. IF AUDIENCE STARTS TO APPLAUD AFTER A GAG: Please! I'd rather not be obligated. HECKLERS: I know you're not a North-woods hunter. THEY only open their traps three times a year . . . or . . . Hecklers make me feel like an elevator operator. It isn't the ups and downs that bother me it's the JERKS. HUMOROUS VIEWS OF THE NEWS: I read where Khrushchev received a cable from the Congo, please send us more communist agents, the last batch was delicious.

On balance, British joke vendors, advertising in *Stage,* offered routines at much more reasonable prices than Glason. I was particularly attracted by two skits listed in Jo Hoyle's catalogue. 'REJUVENATION. This is about an oldish man who is married to a wife much younger than himself. She persuades him to have an operation so that he will become young again. This is an original treatment of an old theme. Clean. There is nothing vulgar about it. 5 shillings.' The other was 'TWO OF A KIND. By a strange coincidence, father and son are in love with the same girl. Clean. Plays five minutes. 4 shillings.' John Slattery, yet another joke writer, sent me 25 gags for a pound, as well as a kind personal letter telling me how difficult it was to break in a new act nowadays.

The most high-pressured, hard-sell, and prolific of the various gag writers I contacted was Peter Cagney. The incomparable Cagney. Before driving down to visit Cagney in Hove I answered his ad in *Stage* (20,000 LAUGHS)! and sent him five pounds for an assortment of jokes and routines. Immediately Mr. Cagney, who tailors gags for the individual comic, wrote to ask whether my STYLE was CHEEKY or SLOW-WITTED. He asked for photographs and tape-recordings of my voice. In his MEMO FROM THE GAG FACTORY FOREMAN, Cagney wrote, 'Entertainers everywhere have come to rely on Cagney's – *their* success is *our* bread and butter. We welcome all comedians . . . whether you need one brilliant topical gag or a complete 30 minute television situation comedy series, we can meet the demand with expertise and rapidity, and guarantee a top TAM rating!' On another page in the catalogue, Cagney runs testimonials from satisfied stars such as Bebe Daniels & Ben Lyons ('Thank you for the fine scripts'), Ken Dodd ('Great material'), Max Miller ('Excellent'), and Dick Haynes ('Made the show'). He also claims to have written material for THE WORLD'S GREAT COMICS in Brazil, aboard the *Queen Mary,* in Ghana, Bermuda, and Canada. GET IN THE SWIM, he urges. HIT THE HIGH-SPOTS. USE ONLY BRILLIANT CAGNEY COMEDY! 'NO OTHER scriptwriters in the world have such a magnificent and widespread record of assignments . . . our writers are ALSO established and well-known novelists – two of them under contract to Herbert Jenkins Ltd., Kometforlaget (Stockholm), Cité de la Presse (Paris) and publishers in Spain, U.S.A., Germany, and Portugal. THE ONLY OTHER WAY WE CAN CONVINCE YOU THAT WE ARE TRULY THE BEST, IS TO BLEED FOR YOU . . . AND THIS CAN *ALSO* BE ARRANGED. A Comedian's success is 60% his script. Invest in YOURSELF – *today*!'

The bundle I got from Cagney included a spill of familiar jokes (Do you know who is the lightweight champion of our town? Our grocer.), 'breast jokes and variations on familiar breast jokes.' I also received a copy of the M.C.'s COMPLETE ALBUM FOR DANCES AND PARTIES, fully copyrighted and available in seven languages like the rest of Cagney's material. One Party Game highly recommended by Cagney is the STRIP JACK NAKED ELIMINATION. 'The MC calls for garments to be removed by the male partner at each break. Sooner or later some men will voluntarily quit but the best of them will go on to the end. Start with necktie, tunic collars and belts, braces, etc. Do NOT go beyond reasonable bounds! For fun, a stooge might be planted in the contest, wearing highly-coloured tartan football knickers, and this one might remove his trousers when all others have been eliminated. Give prize to genuine winner, of course.'

Peter Cagney, lean, nervy and forty-six years old, told me that he has been a writer for thirty years. Cagney is not only a comedy writer. He has written novels, thrillers, stories, and musicals, and for a while after the war he published his own magazine, STAG.

'Eventually they all come to me,' Cagney said. 'There's nobody who can compete with me for comedy writing today –'

'What about... Simpson and Galton?'

'Simpson and Galton! What did they do before they wrote comedy? They were amateurs. Did you see that double page spread on Simpson and Galton in the *Express* or the *Mail*? It shows one of them lying on a sofa and the other half asleep in a chair... and it says, Portrait of Two Comedy Writers thinking. *Thinking!* Who has time to think? I can write a thirty minute television script, complete with technical details, in twenty minutes. *I'm* a professional.... There's nobody who can compete with me for comedy writing today. I get all sorts of calls, you know. From somebody making a speech at the boiler-makers' dinner who needs a few cracks to a complete thirty minute script for Swedish TV. I've done the lot.'

Cagney pointed out a glassed-in bookcase to me.

'I've written forty million words – 78 books – you'd think I'd have made a bloody fortune, wouldn't you? I mean those words aren't stuff that's gone into the wastepaper basket. Published. The lot. Then you take somebody like John Braine, he writes one flipping book – it's serialised in the *Express* and he's made. Amateurs. Colin Wilson can't even spell. I've got a letter from him, did you know? Braine writes one book – a flash in the pan, isn't it? I mean for authorship. That's what I stand for. I've written 78 books – no, 84. Unless it's a property – a bound book – there's no future in it. Now look,' he said, hitting the bookcase, 'I'd back any of these books – any of them – against what-his-name – that geezer Fleming. He made a fortune. A load of cod's wallop it was too.'

I asked Cagney if he still wrote books.

'No. I had a contract with Herbert Jenkins, four books a year, but what with all the other work I do it was taking me something like eight weeks to get rid of them. So I had to give it up, the novels, it was crippling. The flaming agent takes 30 per cent, you know, and even with the translations I was only earning an average of £300 a book. . . . Once,' Cagney said, slumping on the sofa, 'Columbia pictures was going to buy twelve of them. . . .'

'What happened?'

'Well, it fell through.'

Cagney told me he only earns about £20 a week, after expenses. He has three children.

'Have you ever thought of giving it up?' I asked.

'You're always waiting for the lucky break. It's sheer luck, you know. Simpson and Galton – they're lazy. I do more work in three weeks than they do in a year. I write for working men's clubs and holiday camps, that's a market the big money boys ignore, isn't it?'

Peter Cagney has been a joke writer since 1952. He has, he

told me, some 2,000 regular clients and about 100 of them buy material from him on a monthly basis. Last year Cagney's catalogue of STAG GAGS, CLUBLAND SPECIALS, VISI-GAGS, PATTER PARADES, and COMEDY ACTS made for a turnover of about £1,500.

Had he ever tried London, I asked.

'London? It's a closed shop. I mean TV, it's a closed ring, isn't it? There must be 20,000 comedy writers in this country, but if you look over 15 years' copies of the *Radio Times* I'll bet you don't find twenty new names. Look,' Cagney said, 'you tell me, what's the best comedy show on TV?'

'Well, I –'

'*The Beverley Hillbillies*. And I can do better. I know from the testimonials I get that I could write a better show than any on the air. But it's a closed shop at the BBC. It should be investigated. Muir and Norden, now they're not professionals. That isn't authorship. Whoever heard of them before they were well-known?'

GAMES (SOME) PEOPLE PLAY

More bad news. Five, maybe six, years ago, an outspoken American published a book about indigenous homosexuals with the title *Every Third Man*, and this spring, from Bryan Magee, we have *One In Twenty*,[1] a treatment of the same problem in Little England. Even allowing for American hyperbole and British understatement the gap, I must say, is intolerable. It suggests that this sinking island has fallen behind in yet another field, fallen *very far* behind when you consider that Mr. Magee's statistics include lesbians, butch and femme.

On the plus side, Mr. Magee's one in twenty statistic, though questionable, has the singular merit of being above mean party politics. That is to say, this statistic differs from all others hurled at us in 1966 in that it is not related to those notorious thirteen wasted years of Toryism. We are not told if one in twenty represents a shrinkage or if, given the smack of firm government, we can hope for an upward trend round the corner. I shall leave it to more committed journals, say *Tribune* and the *Spectator*, to tell us if the one in twenty figure represents a decline, and shall confine myself here to com-

[1] London, Secker & Warburg Ltd., 1966.

menting on the literary and social merits of Bryan Magee's book.

One In Twenty has had, on balance, a favourable press, which is astonishing because, though the study is not badly meant, it is surely one of the worst-written, unintentionally funny, books I've ever read. To begin with, it is choked with clichés. A random sampling unearths . . . at the drop of a hat, on the fingers of one hand, in their heart of hearts, skeleton in the cupboard. Sex tends to rear 'its ugly head' and emotions, wouldn't you know, are 'bottled up.' Bryan Magee, undoubtedly sensitive to the real and imagined problems of a sexual minority group, has no feeling whatsoever for language, which is rather a ruinous shortcoming in a writer. Even a writer of grey, obvious sociology. To be fair, Mr. Magee is primarily a TV commentator – this book grew out of two probing, outspoken *This Week* documentaries – and as such he can transmogrify dry if questionable fact into living tabloid prose. 'The fact that one person in twenty is homosexual means that we must not be surprised if we find, on average, something like one homosexual in every large family, and several homosexuals in every street.'

Mr. Magee has a rare gift for truisms. 'Homosexuality,' he writes as early as page twenty-seven, 'almost certainly has not one cause but many causes.' A trained observer, he soon adds 'There is a marginal tendency for homosexuals to drift into those occupations and professions which are more tolerant of homosexuals and away from those which are less.' Continuing in the same daring, original manner, he equates homosexuals with other minority groups: Jews and Negroes. 'Jewishness and colour,' he observes astutely, 'go in families, but the homosexual is usually the only one in his family.' Developing this thought some, he adds, 'colour is always – and Jewishness usually – self-evident, whereas homosexuality is hidden' and concludes, 'To be a practising Jew is not a crime, but to be a practising male homosexual is.' If there is not a word here for special cases, say self-evident Jews who are hidden homosexuals (are they allowed to play golf at gentile homosexual country clubs?), he is not without compassion for the children of homosexuals. 'For a mother to go lesbian,' he writes, 'is felt as an extreme form of rejection by the son.'

Life, as seen by Bryan Magee, is no bowl of cherries for the homosexual. 'They cannot sit on a park bench kissing each other, or walk down the street hand in hand, or embrace on a railway platform,' all of which suggests that London, after all, may not be the world's most swinging city.

All the chapters in *One In Twenty* have flat, C. P. Snow-like headings. 'Can Homosexuals Change?' 'What Do Lesbians Do?' 'My Personal Attitude.' One of my favourite chapters, 'What Are the Advantages For a Man Being Homosexual?', deals with certain built-in perks to homosexuality, practical perks. Homosexual couples, Mr. Magee writes, tend to have no baby-sitting problems and more money to spend. They are not usually burdened by such heterosexual curses as mortgages and putting money aside for the children's education. And yet – and yet – they face loneliness in middle-age: there are no children. But, I ask in a spirit of reform, is this necessary? *Really necessary?* Couldn't this problem be solved if enough forward-looking, liberal-minded people were willing to campaign for a homosexual adoption society?

If Mr. Magee's study is redeemed by more than one touch of unconscious humour, it is (would-be readers be warned) essentially pompous. On a trip to Holland, where homosexuality between consenting adults is no crime, the author relates that he visited a Dutch organization for homosexuals of both sexes. He finds nothing amusing in that this organization is called C.O.C. (short for 'Cultuur-en Ontspanningscentrum'). 'The C.O.C.,' he writes, 'struck me as an organization that does good,' and by George he's got something there. But one must persevere until the latter pages of this study to find anything controversial. For it is only on page 137 that Bryan Magee, in the true publish and be damned spirit, comes right out and says, 'Female sexuality is different from male sexuality: women's bodies are different from men's, their sexual functions are different. . . .' The mind boggles. It was at this point in fact that I skipped to read the jacket blurb, looking for and finding reassurance. The man who has written that women's bodies are different from men's has not only been to Oxford, where he took two degrees and was president of the Union, but he has held a Fellowship in Philosophy at Yale and has served with British Military Intelligence in Central Europe. He must know what he's talking about.

NOT ME, LEARY, NOT ME

Make no mistake. Billy Graham and Tim Leary are running in the same soul-claiming race, the former betting only Christ can save, the latter, chemistry. Messiah, martyr, and high priest of the psychedelic, Leary writes that he was, until 1960, 'a 40-year-old-smart-alec atheist at Harvard,' a research psychologist, when his mind was blown by the sacred mushroom (psilocybin), morning-glory seeds, nutmeg, marijuana, peyote, mescalin, and, above all, LSD, sweeping him 'over the edge of a sensory Niagara into a maelstrom of transcendental visions and hallucinations.'

Leary has since taken the LSD trip more than three hundred times, his appetite just possibly whetted by a pioneering voyage into inner space, wherein, among other illuminations, it was revealed to him that he 'may well be one of the wisest men born before 1945.' Nice, very nice, for Tim, but it does create problems in my earthbound mind. Leary's primary claim is that LSD is mind-expanding, more nourishing for our kids than porridge. Being a non-tripper, I can't say for sure. But what arouses my suspicions is that if Leary found LSD so incredibly mind-expanding, he had, on the evidence of the book to hand, the decidedly unfair advantage of there being so much room to begin with.

The Politics of Ecstasy[1] is a grab-bag of lectures, interviews, and articles, often glib, sometimes plausible, and charged everywhere with irresponsible, even dangerous, pronouncements. Turn on, tune in, drop out, writes Leary, a born deviser of catchphrases and headlines, seldom lingering long enough to qualify his declarations with substantiating arguments. Are we to take it as writ, for instance, that 'In 5,000 million years the sun's supply of hydrogen will be burned up; the planets will be engulfed with a final solar explosion,' when, given moon rock for the first time, our scientists are so engagingly split as to its actual meaning? And Leary's text is choked with such inflated cosmic opinions and wild claims, all presented as unchallengeable verities.

Shorn of his inflations, Leary, like you and me, is scared of dying, but has found a transcendental security blanket in the insight that we are all one and deathless, being comprised of energy, a dance of particles, with the added benefit of cellular memory, going back to the pre-Cambrian slime, which can only be summoned up on an LSD trip. Well, maybe. But again and again the home movies Leary brings back from inner space are as boring as any my Aunt Ida has shot in Israel, as well as being self-regarding, stale and simple-minded. We all want to know why we are here, he writes, and who we are, and then he returns with the news: 'At the atomic level I am a galaxy of nuclear-powered atoms spinning through changing patterns. I am the universe, the centre and guardian temple of all energy. I am God of Light. Who am I? I'm you.' To which I can only answer, hell, no, Leary, you're not me.

As with Allen Ginsberg, Richard Neville, and others, a good deal is made of the obligatory trip to India, where *karma* is possible, but there is no mention of the mundane fact that *karma* has also made for millions of Untouchables, their sins having been committed in a previous incarnation. Seemingly, even in the soaring beautiful psychedelic world to come, there will be Negroes.

[1] London, MacGibbon & Kee Ltd., 1970.

On the other hand, LSD cannot be all bad if it allows women several hundred orgasms in one loving session and has multiplied Leary's sexual fun a thousand-fold. In the nick of time, it would appear, for Leary, by his own confession a charismatic public figure, 'does generate attraction and stimulate response. Every woman has built into her cells and tissues the longing for a hero, sage-mythic male, to open up and share her divinity.'

Each charismatic politician flatters his own constituency. Richard Nixon, the silent and middle-aged majority; Leary, the young, who, he writes, with the help of LSD, have already experienced more than Buddha or Einstein, and are indeed the wisest and holiest generation this world has ever seen.

Having once proffered an uneasy apology for being thirty, Richard Neville, editor of OZ would seem to agree. *Play Power*,[2] his exploration of the underground or youthquake, is at once spirited, informative, and clearly the work of an engaging and concerned man. But his testimony is also most exasperating and vitiated by too many half-truths, facile condemnations, and sheer bigotry.

Celebrating the young for being naturally endowed with what old and now largely unread Hemingway once proscribed as essential equipment for any writer – a built-in shit-detector – he ventures nothing will ever be the same any more. Elitist-culture, Eliot, Yeats, Wordsworth, *et al*, will be swept away, and deservedly, it would seem, for 'Nazis wept over Wagner then turned on the gas.' The mind boggles. For Sir Cyril Black could readily reply that the Moors murderers read de Sade, and he should therefore be banned, and I could chip in, perversely, Adolf Hitler favoured a macrobiotic diet and did his thing, as we all know, and consequently was a flower child.

Of course pot should be legalised. I agree that universities are too intricately involved with the military-industrial complex, but I part with Neville over what he takes to be the untarnished beauty of all student uprisings. Some are mindless,

[2] London, Jonathan Cape, Ltd., 1970.

others, brutalised. Which is to say, I don't think it entirely beautiful to defecate in a dean's filing cabinet or tear to shreds a history professor's notes of twenty years.

If I understand Neville correctly, his essential argument is that the international youth rebellion terrifies the rest of us, and their so-called new culture is 'alive, exciting, fun, ephemeral, disposable, unified, unpredictable, uncontrollable, lateral, organic, and popular.' Furthermore, the young were born into a world where work is considered ennobling, unlike the ancient Greeks for whom a life of leisure was essential and work was considered degrading, something to be done by slaves. In the new order, all work will be done for fun and every night will be Saturday night.

Well, yes. I am terrified, but largely because this wilfully uninformed generation thinks things are happening for the first time and, whilst professing love and mind-expansion, they are as bigoted as Colonel Blimp.

Years ago, Hemingway suggested the trouble with Henry Miller was that having once been fucked in the afternoon he thought he had invented it. Similarly, the hippies fail to grasp that ten years before them there were the beats and, in my time, long-haired sandalled kids were called existentialists. Before that they were merely bohemians and along there was pot and, *pace* Jerry Rubin, revolution for the hell of it.

What scares me about this generation is the extent to which ignorance is their armour. If no-nothingness goes on much longer somebody will yet emerge from a commune having discovered . . . the wheel. Meanwhile, we have as an appendix to Neville's book, *Free London*, something adapted from 'Project London,' a manual the publishers take to be so subversive they 'wish to stress they in no way condone either the contents . . . or its spirit.'

Give, give.

But all you discover therein is that you can snooze free in Harrod's banking hall and that the way to get into the cinema without paying is to have a friend open the emergency exit.

In a word, the sort of lore known to working-class kids from Montreal to Liverpool for generations.

As fierce reactionaries utterly condemn long-haired hippies as layabouts, drug-addicts, and perverts, uniformly in need of the lash, so Neville dismisses all so-called 'straights' out-of-hand. 'The new communalism reacts against Western style family "units" and their seedy invention of old people's homes, mother-in-law hatred, baby sitters and baby bashers. The bank manager's ideal family isolates one from another, ill-preparing its offspring for relating to the outside world. Love thy neighbour – so long as he is safely ensconced within his capsule; But the revolutionary young are also sadly ensconced within a restricting capsule, on the evidence not so much liberated as having settled for the dark underside of the middle-class coin, both groups with their minds closed to culture.

There are some amusing ironies too. Whereas the bank manager's wife might regret they no longer write good novels like Maugham's *The Razor's Edge* or Hilton's *Lost Horizons,* I can see these, after Leary, as seminal books for a youth-worshipping generation that so sentimentalises the East.

Finally, there is the work problem, wherein Neville is guilty of over-simplification and a certain duplicity. Going back to ancient Greece, my fear is I would have been one of the slaves, you would have had the life of leisure, but let it pass, let it pass. Naturally, most work is demeaning; it is also insufficiently rewarding. Furthermore, poverty brutalises, which is why I remain a socialist. But if we can look forward to a future of play, wafted thereto on computerised wings, we will owe our liberty not to Neville or me, scribblers both, but to the 'straights' everywhere.

Writing *Play Power* had to be hard work as well as fun. Neville is not giving it away on street corners, but selling it through bookshops. It is a deeply felt and honourable book, but Neville has also written it seeking recognition and profit. Having allowed his publisher to send it out for review, I assume he would rather it was acclaimed than deprecated. Not yet thirty-one, he is already a competitor. I am not reproaching him for this, merely asking him to recognise it.

FOLLOWING THE BABYLONIAN TALMUD, AFTER MAIMONIDES...

Rabbi Stuart Rosenberg on the History of the Jewish Community in Canada

If Rabbi Stuart Rosenberg, sole begetter of *The Jewish Community in Canada*,[1] Volume 1, a History, had instead undertaken to write an account of the assassination of John Kennedy it would have run as follows:

'President John F. Kennedy (who was boosted in his campaign for office by such Jewish luminaries as Norman Mailer, of writing-fame, Senator Abe Ribicoff, and Danny Kaye, of film-fame) drove into Dallas on Nov. 22, 1963. Dallas, it is worth noting, was the birthplace of Izzy Lubin, the first Jew to be arrested for jay-walking in Macon County. The city is no more than 300 miles from Houston, the setting for Neiman-Marcus, of department store-fame, and home of the Chevra Kadisha congregation, president Benjy Taub. Indispensable community leaders are Hy Green, Sam Farber, Mort Weiner, the Fiedler family, and Norm Levi.

'Tooling into downtown Dallas, which welcomes Jewish shopkeepers, among them Sid's Deli, President Kennedy rode in an open Lincoln Continental, a Ford product. The Ford

[1] Toronto, McClelland & Stewart, Limited, 1971.

Company is not ashamed to advertise in *Commentary* and numbers many of our brethren among its distributors, not to say, share-holders, most of whom support the annual Israeli Bond drive, the Red Cross, Mother's Day, and oil depletion allowances. As the car passed the Texas Public School Book Depository, with lots of titles by Jewish authors in stock, somebody called Oswald shot and killed Kennedy.

'A day to remember!

'And, I am now free to reveal, that among the crowd who will remember there was a goodly sprinkling of Jews, prominent among them, the Shapiros of San Antonio; Barney Kugler, a descendant of the first Jewish postmaster of Waco; and Seymour Freed, the distinguished past treasurer of the United Jewish Appeal in Shreveport and a wholesale gunsmith whose cultural contribution to that proud city is second to none!

'Oswald, not a Jew himself, numbered among his acquaintances one Jack Ruby, who was to shoot him dead in turn, though not on the sabbath. A report was issued following the assassination and shoot-up, the so-called Warren Commission Report, though the real digging was done by counsellors David Bellin, Melvin Eisenberg, Arlen Spector, and Alfred Goldberg, with somebody called O'Brien to empty the ashtrays.'

In other words, what Rabbi Rosenberg has wrought is not so much a history as a catalogue, ostensibly boring, but inadvertently hilarious. Writing in the language of Shakespeare, as well as that of the Geritol commercial, the author owes something to Polonius, even more to the school of failed advertising copy writers. But his compendium, to be fair, radiates generosity. For if, as Rabbi Rosenberg claims, there are some 280,000 Jews in Canada, then it seems that at least half of them are enshrined in the history, and even to be mentioned by the rabbi is to be fulsomely praised. The author, whatever else can be held against him, has a heart of gold. If, for instance, he had cast his perceptive eye on Jack Ruby what would have been revealed was a dedicated social worker, especially concerned with the lot of itinerant strippers and underpaid, thirsty cops.

True, an ungracious nit-picker might question the Rabbi's system of values and the relevance, beyond their undisputed office as potential book-buyers, of the plethora of names mentioned, as well as some serious omissions. That is to say, if Karl Marx had been a Canadian-born rather than a German Jew, his name would not have been enscribed in the history unless, like Sydney Maislin, Ben Beutel, or Maxwell Cummings, he was one of 'a handful of leaders who could be regarded as wielders of wide and crucial powers in the life and direction of Montreal Jewry.' Similarly, Franz Kafka, arguably a born out-patient, would not have rated an entry, unless he had been appointed to the board of governors of the Jewish General Hospital.

Given the abundantly dramatic, even ennobling, story of that heroic generation of Jews who came to Canada steerage, largely penniless, without English or French, to gather scrap in alleys, peddle shoelaces, and teach socialist doctrine on the Canadian steppes (some of them succumbing to penury in basement tailor shops, others, with an eye on the main chance, emerging as robber-barons, poets, fabled bootleggers, gamblers, wizards financial or medical), it has been Rabbi Rosenberg's uncommon achievement to render their history bland as frozen processed peas, no colour tolerated unless it be artificial.

Here, for instance, is how he disposes of the rise of the Bronfmans. 'One of the major incidents in Montreal history in the 1880s took place, interestingly enough, over two thousand miles west of the city. Yehiel Bronfman and his wife moved from Bessarabia, Russia, to Wampella, Saskatchewan, one of the first members of the Jewish farm colony established there. Later moving to Brandon and finally to Winnipeg, Bronfman was to father eight children, of which his four sons – Abe, Harry, Sam, Allan – were to become millionaire financiers, philanthropists and major leaders of Jewish causes in Montreal in the following century.' Thereby reducing a tale, the natural material of Isaac Babel, to absolutely nothing.

Though there is hardly a nondescript alderman or community pillar from coast-to-coast who is not hailed in the history, there is no mention made of Fred Rose, the communist MP, or his trial, actually the first of the post-war atom-bomb trials. Montrealers, especially, will be astonished to discover that, amidst so many nonentities blessed, there was also no space for Michael Buhay, a more engaging communist politician, or that fabulous gambler of the late Forties, Harry Ship. Neither is there a word spoken on behalf of our boyhood sports hero, boxer Maxie Berger. Good enough to enter the ring with Ike Williams, but obviously not the stuff to fire the Rabbi's imagination, any more than that good local featherweight Louis Alter, who once fought Willie Pep.

This is not to suggest that *The Jewish Community in Canada* is officiously polite, a snowjob, or that it only celebrates the bland. In the age of the common man, a commonplace book. No, no. The shattering truth is that the author, ostensibly our people's PR supreme, has disturbed a hive laden with honey for anti-Semites.

The first Jewish settler in Canada, Rabbi Rosenberg reveals, was not, as Bruce McKelvie, an authority on British Columbia history, has ventured, a wandering Chinese hassid-cum-prospector, a member of one of the ten tribes lost in Babylonian captivity, staking a claim to Victoria as early as 2,000 B.C. No. The first Jewish settler, Esther Brandeau, was a transvestite. Anticipating Myra Breckinridge, she arrived in 1738, disguised as a man and going by the name of Jacques La Farge. Even more compromising news. Many years before Steinberg's had even been dreamed of, the miracle marts to both Generals Montcalm and Wolfe were Jewish-owned. Montcalm's foodstuffs were supplied by one M. Abe Grandis and Wolfe, a comparison-shopper, learned to depend on Sir Alexander Schomberg. More gratifyingly, Rabbi Rosenberg reveals that the very first Jewish writer in Canada was a man called Mordecai. He was, in fact, the incomparable Adolphus Mordecai Hart, author of *Practical Suggestions on Mining Rights and Privileges in Lower Canada*, a seminal chunk of Canadiana too long out of print.

The author, no pussyfoot, is most rewarding on our city, Montreal, Montreal, which he comes right out and claims as ... The Capital of Jewish Canada, and that, sir, is what I call standing up to René Lévesque and other French Canadian squatters. 'The social life of the Jews of Montreal over the past century,' Rabbi Rosenberg writes with his accustomed assurance, 'has centred around its "clubs". The two most worthy of note are the Montefiore and the de Sola.'

The social life of the very rich, perhaps, but not of the majority of the Jewish populace. Indeed, I could argue, citing names and accomplishments, a much better case for the informal gatherings that were once held at Wilensky's Cigar & Soda, corner of Fairmount and St. Urbain, and that the most distinguished Jews ever to emerge from Montreal were shaped on the playing fields of Baron Byng High School; our Eton. But I would feel miserable, considering how good-hearted the Rabbi is, to end on a sour note. He is, above all, to be prized as a man who has taken 280,000 Jews to his bosom and found only beautiful things to say about all of them. I, for one, would be unable to do as much for an equal number of Protestants or Catholics. On the other hand, washing our Jews whiter than the purest snow, sanitizing them, as it were, it is also possible Rabbi Rosenberg has dehumanized a truly compelling bunch, whose colourful history has yet to be written.

Wait, wait. This is only the first volume of Rabbi Rosenberg's testimonial, and it ends with a rhetorical question. 'In Canada, Jews have come a long way, and more specifically, in a very, very short time: since World War II. But will material achievements diminish their cultural and spiritual possibilities? Will success spoil them?

'We turn our attention to this theme, in the volume that follows. Can Jews and Judaism flourish and grow in the midst of freedom?'

Watch this space.

MAPLE LEAF CULTURE TIME

Twenty-odd years ago, when I was an adolescent zoot-suiter in Montreal, our most revered radio disc jockey's signature tune began, 'It's make-believe ballroom time, the hour of sweet romance.' Today we are well into an even sweeter hour of Canadian romance, maple leaf culture time, an era at once embarrassingly grandiose, yet charged with promise. We are smitten with an unseemingly hasty tendency to count and codify, issuing definitive anthologies of 100 years of poetry and prose and fat literary anthologies, as if by cataloguing we can make it real, by puffing, meaningful, especially if mere publication is taken as a licence to enshrine the most ephemeral stuff, as witness the following entry in *The Oxford Companion to Canadian History and Literature*[1]:

> Beresford-Howe, Constance Elizabeth (1922–) Born in Montreal . . . she is the author of several historical romances. These include . . . *My Lady Greensleeves* (1955), based on an Elizabethan divorce case, in which she shows a sound command of historical detail.

[1] Norah Story, *The Oxford Companion to Canadian History and Literature* (Toronto, Oxford University Press, 1967).

What characterises Canadian culture today is not so much energy and talent – though it is there at last, a real but tender shoot – as an astonishing affluence and beneficence. Happily, an enlightened beneficence. But as the British health plan, in its formative years, could be sniped at by reactionaries, for handing out toupées to all comers, so our culture plan is vulnerable to the charge of staking just about all the alienated kids to committing their inchoate, but modish, complaints to paper or canvas. On the other hand, betting on fragile promise is a built-in hazard of art investment and the people who run the Canada Council could hardly be more decent and imaginative. It's a pity, then, that the Council's first eleven years could come to be noted for one conspicuous omission. Morley Callaghan has yet to be presented with its highest award, the Molson Prize.[2]

Which brings me to our ludicrous, newly-minted honours system, an innovation that must be seen as the last snobbish gasp of our eldest generation, the unselective, slavish Anglophiles. Really, in these austerity-minded days it's high time the Queen dismissed her Canadian second-floor maid, the Governor-General, who is of course Chancellor of the Order of the Companions of Canada, which now entitles many a bore to write the initials 'CC' after his name, a measure hitherto accorded only to bottles of medicine. But my immediate point is, once more Morley Callaghan was overlooked. And then insulted. For, on second thought it seems, he was asked to accept the also-ran Medal of Canada.

Meanwhile, lesser writers, all of them world-famous in Canada, are blowing the dust off early manuscripts and digging old letters out of the attic, mindful of the burgeoning market in raw Canadiana. Book-length studies of just about everybody in the house are threatened, operas are being commissioned, ballet companies subsidised, and townships sorely in need of tolerable restaurants and bars are being paid to erect theatres instead. If Canada was once loosely stitched together by rail-

[2] Callaghan was in fact awarded the Molson Prize in 1970.

roads, such is the force of today's culture-boom that it may be reknit by art palaces coast-to-coast, though there hardly be plays or players, not to mention audiences, to fill them. The promise of a Canadian film industry, backed by ten million dollars, alarms me for other reasons.

Even as in London, the movies have become increasingly, almost insufferably, fashionable among younger Canadian writers, intellectuals, and students. In fact, the sort of student who once used to help put out a snarling little magazine, everything in lower-case letters, writing poems about his revolt against crippling poverty, is nowadays more likely to be making a film with a hand-held camera, all about his rebellion against suffocating affluence.

The dizzying prospect of a Canadian film industry frightens me when I dig into my own past experience of Toronto-based production companies. The archetypal Toronto film outfit has made indecently large profits out of TV commercials or has perhaps produced a puerile but money-spinning series about Indians or mounties, and has now set its sights higher, so to speak. They wish to make a 'serious, yet commercially viable' film *with Canadian content*. That is to say, if *The Young Wantons* will look yet again at sex (unblinkingly, frankly, outspokenly) this time out it will be set in the palpitating streets of LSD-crazed, hippie-ridden, wife-swapping, transvestite-rich Toronto. Ontary-ary-ary-yo; with French Canadian tits being given equal exposure.

Junk is junk, and there would be no honour in Canada adding to the pile. Given our inexperience it is in the nature of things that our junk would be inferior to the glossy Hollywood or London product. We no more require a film industry for its own sake than the emergent African states need their costly airlines. On the evidence of last year's art film, the appalling *Waiting for Caroline,* co-sponsored by our two worthies, the CBC and the National Film Board, we would be well advised to wait a bit longer before plunging into a programme of feature film production, lest premature activity set us back even further.

If the arts in Canada were neglected, today, such is our longing, they are being rushed into shouldering a significance not yet justified by fulfilment. The proliferating anthologies, summaries, and histories vary enormously in quality. The handsomely produced *Modern Canadian Verse*,[3] a bilingual anthology edited by A. J. M. Smith, represents our established poets intelligently and introduces a number of lively young voices. It is a collection for which it would be foolish to make extravagant claims, but it can be offered without apology. Increasingly, Canadian poets (Irving Layton and Leonard Cohen are a case in point) are finding an astonishingly large audience.

Among last year's centennial spill of short story anthologies, *Modern Canadian Stories*[4] promised to be refreshingly different if only because it was edited by foreigners, Giose Rimanelli and Roberto Ruberto. In a foreword, Earle Birney writes of Rimanelli, a new name to me, that he is one of Italy's important men-of-letters, a prize-winning author of novels and short stories, a leading playwright and film writer. But instead of new, yet provocative, judgments, the editors, for the most part, fall back on familiar stories and writers (Leacock, Callaghan, Ethel Wilson, even Mazo de la Roche), for which I do not blame them, as possibilities are still limited. What I do reproach Rimanelli and Ruberto for is a Polonius-like introduction:

> Literature is not a mere word, but the individual expression of man's spirit. Consequently, to study the literature of an epoch means to study the spirit of the man of that epoch. Man lives, thinks, and acts. . . .

Which introduction finally comes unstuck through simple arithmetic ('at least five other Canadian writers deserve

[3] Toronto, Oxford University Press, 1968.
[4] Toronto, Ryerson Press, 1968.

mention here: Jack Ludwig, Norman Levine, Dave Godfrey, and Sheila Watson'). More seriously, Mavis Gallant, our most compelling short story writer since Callaghan, is not included.

Neither is Mavis Gallant included among the more than 350 entries in *Canadian Writers/Ecrivains Canadiens*,[5] a biographical dictionary edited by Guy Sylvestre, Brandon Conron, and Carl F. Klinck, whilst my listing manages a grammatical error and a new, yet provocative judgment in one sentence. 'In addition to his novels, Richler ... worked on the film script for John Osborne's *Room At The Top* and *Life At The Top*.'

Norah Story's *Oxford Companion to Canadian History and Literature*, with 2,000 separate articles, 9 pages of maps, 2,300 cross-references, and a list of titles for more than 6,000 books, is at once more scholarly, even definitive. I have no quarrel with it as a historical reference, but as a literary guide it suffers from perfunctory, fact-bound summaries. It honours quantity rather than quality, so that many a dreary lending-library novelist is dealt with at length, but there is no individual entry for Adele Wiseman, author of only one novel, *The Sacrifice*. It's not so much a literary who's who as an all-inclusive directory.

A more ambitious, perceptive study is the *Literary History of Canada*,[6] edited by Carl F. Klinck, Claude Bissell, Roy Daniells, Northrop Frye, and others. This volume, eight years in the making, is, in fact, a study of Canadian literature in English and will be followed by a *Histoire de la littérature canadienne-française*. Happily, the *History* is not only comprehensive, but it is informed by wit and sensibility; it dares judgments and strives for critical balance. A balance that is necessarily protective at times, but never tainted by culture-rousing chauvinism. 'The book is a tribute,' Northrop Frye writes in his 'Conclusion,' 'to the maturity of Canadian literary scholarship and criticism, what ever one thinks of the literature.'

---

[5] Toronto, Ryerson Press, 1968.
[6] Toronto, University of Toronto Press, 1968.

Non-Canadian readers familiar with Professor Frye's larger body of work are perhaps unaware of his especial Canadian office. Among so many uncritical celebrators, he, like Leavis here, like Trilling in New York, is our keeper of true standards. Had the evaluative view, he writes, based on the conception of criticism as concerned mainly to define and canonise the genuine classics of literature, been the *History*'s guiding principle, 'this book would, if written at all, have been only a huge debunking project.' There is no Canadian writer, he reminds us:

> of whom we can say what we can say of the world's major writers, that their readers grow up inside their work without ever being aware of a circumference.

Yet he allows that the evidence shows 'that the Canadian imagination has passed the stage of exploration and has embarked on settlement' and concludes, 'the writers featured in this book have identified the habits and attitudes of the country, as Fraser and Mackenzie have identified its rivers. They have also left an imaginative legacy of dignity and high courage.'

Professor Frye also notes that such is the obvious and unquenchable desire of the Canadian cultural public to identify itself through its literature that:

> ... there are so many medals offered for literary achievement that a modern Canadian Dryden might well be moved to write a satire on medals, except that if he did he would probably be awarded the medal for satire and humour.

And this, not neglect, it seems to me, is our most dangerous Canadian enemy of promise today.

'ETES-VOUS CANADIEN?'

Early in April, 1969, I discovered I was among the year's Governor-General's Award Winners for literature.

'You're accepting it,' my Canadian publisher said, astonished.

'Yes.'

'You're pleased, you're actually pleased.'

'Yes, I am.'

Several years earlier, a friend of mine had won the award for a collection of essays. At the reception in Government House, Ottawa, his wife, suddenly distressed, drove him into a corner. 'He says he hasn't read it himself, but his maid did and liked it very much.'

'No, no,' my friend assured her 'his *aide* he means his *aide*.'

Traditionally, the GG, the Queen's very own Canadian second floor maid, stands behind two major horse races: the Queen's Plate and the Governor-General's Awards (never more than six) for the best books of the year. Though one Queen's Plate winner, the fabulous Northern Dancer, also came first in the Kentucky Derby, so far no Governor-General's Award winner has ever been entered in the final heat for the Nobel. The first Governor-General's Awards were presented by Lord Tweedsmuir in 1937 to Bertram Brooker and T. B. Robertson, who, it's safe to say, are now remembered for nothing else. Among others who have officially signed the Canadian literary skies with their honour there are John Murray Gibson, Franklin S. McDowell, Alan Sullivan, Winifred Bambrick, William Sclater and R. MacGregor Dawson. I could go on. I could go on and on, seemingly composing a letterhead with names fit to adorn only the most exclusive Montreal or Toronto law office. But, to be fair, in recent years the awards have also been presented to Morley Callaghan and Gabrielle Roy, Hugh MacLennan, Brian Moore, Rejean Ducharme, George Woodcock, Marshall McLuhan and, posthumously, to Malcolm Lowry.

Until 1959, when the Canada Council took over the administration of the awards, the Governor-General forked out 50 guineas to the horse that won the Queen's Plate, but offered just a handshake (royal only by osmosis since Vincent Massey became the first Canadian-born GG in 1952), and a copy of your book signed in his own hand, to writers. The Canada Council, happily cognisant of the stuff that really excites this country's artistic types, tacked a $1,000 purse to the awards in 1959, raising the ante to $2,500 six years later. What had once been a stigma was now inspiring. It was also made respectable, because the Council saw to it that the judge's panel was literate. A new departure, for in years past the incomparable Canadian Authors' Association adjudicated the awards. 'What, who, why, when,' asks an editorial in the Association's *Author and Bookman*, 'is a Canadian writer?'

> If a writer wants to make big money he will probably stop writing about Canada and almost certainly leave Canada. If a writer wants 'instant fame' he will very likely have to prostitute his talent by such things as writing sex-dripping prose or taking a deliberately shocking stand on a touchy subject.

This year's awards created a small uproar. THE ESTAB-LISHMENT BEWARE!, ran the headline in the Toronto *Globe and Mail*, THESE AWARDS ARE WITH IT. Winners for 1968 were Hubert Aquin, for his novel, *Trou de mémoires*, Fernand Dumont, for his sociological work, *Le lieu de l'homme*, and Marie-Claire Blais, for her novel, *Les Manuscrits de Pauline Archange*. English-language writers were Leonard Cohen, for his *Selected Poems*; Alice Munro, for her first book of short stories, *Dance of the Happy Shades*; and me, for *Cocksure*, a novel, and *Hunting Tigers Under Glass*, a collection of essays.

Well now, the truth is we were a scurvy lot. Cohen, who enjoys an immense campus following in Canada and the US, is a self-declared pot smoker. Hubert Aquin, a former vice-president of the militantly separatist RIN party, was once arrested and charged with car theft and being in possession of a revolver. My novel, *Cocksure*, had been banned by the rest of the white commonwealth, not to mention W. H. Smith in the mother country. Aquin, as was to be expected, turned down the award instantly, the GG being anathema to him. Fernand Dumont accepted the award, but two weeks later donated his prize money to the separatist Parti Québecois. Cohen, pondering the inner significance of the award in his hotel in the Village, wavered. He told a Toronto *Star* reporter he wasn't sure whether he would accept the award, it would depend on how he felt when he got up that morning. In the end, he didn't wait that long, but instead issued a statement saying there was much in him that would like to accept the award, but the poems absolutely forbid it.

Another reporter caught up with Cohen in Toronto and asked him, yes, yes, but what, exactly, did he mean?

'Well, I mean they're personal and private poems. With any of my other books I would have been happy to accept, but this one is different. I've been writing these poems since I was 15, and they're very private, their meaning would be changed. And there's another reason. I can't see myself standing up there and accepting the award while there's so much unhappiness in the world, so much violence, while so many of my friends are in jail.'

I accepted the award at once, but with mixed feelings. As a writer I was pleased and richer, but as a father of five, mortified. When *Cocksure* was published in Canada, the reviewer in the Montreal *Star* revealed that I had churned out an obvious potboiler with all the lavatory words. The man who pronounces on books in the New Brunswick *Daily Gleaner* put me down for a very filthy fellow and warned parents in Montreal that I would be teaching their children at Sir George Williams University, where I was to be writer-in-residence for a year. Others denounced me as a pornographer. And now the ultimate symbol of correctitude in our country, the GG himself, would actually reward me for being obscene. For the establishment's sake, I couldn't help but be ashamed.

The Governor-General, I was assured, had read and loathed my novel, but unlike Aquin or Cohen, he did turn up for prizegiving day. Which is not to say he didn't protest. 'The Governor-General is a patron of all the arts, but has little time to master any,' he said. 'But I do have my views, literary as well as political, even though, as in the Speech from the Throne, I have to refrain from expressing them.'

Many Canadians feel the Governor-General is an anomaly; his office, at best, tiresome, at worst, divisive. Not so old Johnny Diefenbaker, who is fond of complaining that Prime Minister Trudeau is an anti-monarchist. Diefenbaker says that before Trudeau became PM, he was asked how he would have voted on a resolution calling for the abolition of the monarchy, and replied: 'If I had been completely logical, I would have abstained because I . . . you know I don't give a damn.' Trudeau has denied this in the House, saying, 'I believe the monarchy is an important symbol to many people. I think more energy would be lost in Canada by debating this subject than would be gained by our institutions.'

My own earliest recollection of the monarchy goes back to the war years when we used to purchase calendars with toothy photographs of Elizabeth and Margaret in their Brownie uniforms. On my way to school every morning I passed another monarchy symbol, the armoury of the Canadian Grenadier Guards and outside, under a funny fur hat, there always stood some tall unblinking *goy*. 'If they were ordered to do it,' I was told, 'they'd march over a cliff. There's discipline for you.'

I have, in my time, lived under seven Governors-General. Only one of them, Lord Tweedsmuir, was abhorrent to me, because under the name of John Buchan he wrote thrillers choked with anti-Semitic nonsense.

Our present Governor-General, however, is hardly the sort to arouse strong feelings. Daniel Roland Michener is an upright, compact little man with curly grey hair and a natty moustache; he has, in this age of rock, the manner of the *maitre d'hotel* in a palm court restaurant. Mrs. Michener, a more obdurate figure, is a case of life improving on the art of Grant Wood. She was born to chaperone the dance in the small town high school gym.

All of us assembled in the reception room at Government House on May 13 rose respectfully when the Micheners, preceded by uniformed aides, drifted in, their smiles frozen; but I, for one, would have found Mr. Michener more credible proffering that large black menu than mounting the dais with such confidence. Behind the Governor-General and his lady, bolstering their acquired royalty as it were, hung enormous portraits of Queen Elizabeth and Prince Philip. The portraits were resoundingly awful, not so much poor likenesses as badly proportioned grotesqueries. Roland Michener, rising to address us, seemed distracted, his manner that of a man who had just come from being photographed accepting a gift of snow shoes from an Eskimo child and must push on to award a Brotherhood plaque to a western mayor in a ten gallon hat, rimless glasses, and high-heeled boots.

The speech Mr. Michener read to us from small cards made for some nervous smiles and at least one giggle from the assembled literati. Observing that all but one of the six award winners were from Quebec, he noted that this might not be a coincidence. 'Politics in Quebec today are tense... social order is in the process of rapid change and upheaval. This is the atmosphere which stirs people to write more and sometimes better, and to produce exciting paintings, sculpture, theatre, and films.'

Alas, the writings of Cohen and Marie-Claire Blais are equally non-political. They have been living in the United States for years, and I am normally rooted in London.

Finally, the award winners were summoned to the Governor-General one by one to accept leather-bound copies of their work signed by Mr. Michener. When my turn came, the Governor-General asked me *'Etes-vous canadien?'*

Startled, I said, *'Oui.'*

He then went on to congratulate me fulsomely in French. *Is it possible,* I thought, appalled, *that the Governor-General is a covert separatist?* If not, why, when I answered yes to his question, had he assumed I was necessarily French-speaking? The mind boggled. In any event, once he was done, I said, *'Merci.'* I did not correct the Governor-General. In my case, it was *noblesse oblige*.

ACKNOWLEDGEMENTS

These essays first appeared, sometimes in a different form, in *Book World, Commentary*, the *Guardian*, the *London Magazine, Maclean's*, the *Montreal Star*, the *Nation, New American Review*, the *New Leader*, the *New Statesman, Saturday Night*, the *Spectator, Town Magazine, Vogue*, and *Works in Progress*.

'Why I Write' reprinted from *Works in Progress*, copyright 1971, The Literary Guild of America Inc.

'A Sense of the Ridiculous' reprinted from *New American Review*, copyright 1968.

'Gordon Craig' reprinted from *Vogue*, copyright 1965.

'Bond' reprinted from *Commentary*, copyright 1968.

'The Holocaust and After' reprinted from the *Spectator*, the *New Leader, Book World,* and the *New Statesman,* copyright 1966, 1968, 1964, and 1969.

'Making It' reprinted from the *Nation*, copyright 1968.

'Huckleberry Finklestone' reprinted from *Book World*, copyright 1965.

'Starting Out in the Thirties' reprinted from *Town Magazine*, copyright 1960.

'Porky's Plaint' reprinted from the *London Magazine*, copyright 1970.

'Answering the Ads' reprinted from *Maclean's*, copyright 1964.

'Games (Some) People Play' reprinted from *Town Magazine*, copyright 1960.

'Not Me, Leary, Not Me' reprinted from the *Guardian*, copyright 1970.

'Following the Babylonian Talmud, After Maimonides...' reprinted from the *Montreal Star*, copyright 1970.

'Maple Leaf Culture Time' reprinted from the *New Statesman*, copyright 1968.

'Êtes-vous canadien?' reprinted from the *New Statesman*, copyright 1969.